BACKPACKER'S COOKBOOK

BACKPACKER'S COOKBOOK

By

Margaret Cross & Jean Fiske

Illustrated by Linda Bennett

TEN SPEED PRESS

ISBN Number 0-913668-15-X

Published by
Ten Speed Press
Box 4310
Berkeley, CA 94704

TABLE OF CONTENTS

This is a book about eating well from your pack. As you walk, moving in rhythm with the land, your body needs simple, satisfying, strength-giving foods. In camp, you don't want to spend very much time cooking, but still you'll look forward to that sense of well-being that comes from being well-fed.

What does it take? A little advance planning and some information about dried foods, essential cooking gear, and your body's real needs.

Within these pages are many of the things we've learned about eating well on our backpacking trips. We'll share with you what we've found out about basic foodstuffs, menu planning, equipment, and many well-worn recipes, as well. At the end of the book is a list of other good books about backpacking, some addresses of mountaineering suppliers, and the names of several mail-order food outfits.

The rest is up to you. Eating well on the trail is not only a matter of facts and methods, it is also a state of mind— a nourishment of spirit that you'll find for yourself, as we have. We can only suggest that you will enter this state of mind more easily, if you pass gently over the land, walking, resting, cooking, but leaving the land undisturbed, as it was before you passed by . . .

BASIC

NOURISHMENT

*But why should not the New Englander try
new adventures . . . ? Why concern ourselves
so much about our beans for seed, and not
be concerned at all about a new generation
of men?*
          —Henry Thoreau, *Walden*

INTAKE
The joy of striding along, at one with trail and sky, is partly
the good feeling of your whole body in harmonious motion.
This steady activity burns many more calories than you use
in city life, especially when the trail is steep, and the pack
heavy. Keeping the joy alive means giving your body the
fuel it needs to work all day and nourishment to build the
new muscles you'll get while hiking.

How much food you'll take, how many calories you'll
need depends on your size, your usual eating habits, and the
amount of activity you plan. For a short, leisurely trip you
may need only 10-20 per cent more than you usually eat.
For a longer, more active trip, try taking about 30 per cent
more. On a push-hard-all-day trip with a heavy pack, or on
a strenuous ski tour or climb, your body may burn 50-75
per cent more calories than you use at home. These and any
other general estimates are useful only as a rule of thumb.
You will determine the diet levels that keep your body happy
through your own experience.

Some weight loss won't be unwelcome if you have pounds to spare, but this is no time to go on a crash diet. Continual hunger will leave you weak and dull, and spoil your enjoyment. Neither is your trip a time to stuff yourself at every chance, although your appetite may soar once it has overcome any initial adjustment problems. Typical hiking food is so rich that a belly continually full may bring indigestion. Too much food in your stomach will interfere with active hiking, climbing and exploring—and that was why you came, wasn't it?

The proteins, carbohydrates, and fats you eat while backpacking will be selected for different virtues than those you normally eat at home, where freshness, delicacy, and perhaps calorie consciousness rule supreme. Your portable pantry will furnish foods that are compact, quick, and easy to fix in your primitive "kitchen," keep very well in heat and dampness, and have a high ratio of calories to weight and bulk.

Carbohydrates are the staple of hikers' diets. They're cheaper than animal protein, usually compact, keep well, digest well. Carbohydrate foods, especially sweets, are quickly converted to energy. A steady supply of carbohydrates in meals and snacks will give your body a fund of energy to draw on while hiking or climbing.

The carbohydrate foods you take can provide you with more food value than just calories if you will search out whole-grain or enriched foods when buying flour, grains, or pasta. Keep this in mind, too, if you buy prepared mixes or one-dish meals. Some are enriched, many are not.

The rigorous conditions of life in your pack tend to reduce light and airy baked goods and cereals to mashed, unappetizing messes or crumbs. A sturdy, dense texture survives best; for instance, take pumpernickel, fruitcake, date bars, farina, wheat thins rather than egg bread, pound-cake, sugar cookies, cornflakes, potato chips.

Proteins at home come primarily from animal sources for most of us: fresh meats (including poultry and fish), milk products, eggs. The latter two are widely available dried, and are excellent sources of protein for hikers.

Meat is usually less prominent in hikers' diets, though. Canned meat is too heavy and bulky for long trips, and freeze-dried meats and jerky are expensive. Salami and other sausages are also expensive when you consider that they contain more fat than protein. Fishing trips are an exception; they can be well-supplied with protein if the fisherman is successful.

During your trip you will want to eat enough protein to keep your muscles in good repair and to accommodate their tendency to grow through sustained exercise. "Enough" varies with your size and age, but for adults .015 oz. (.42 gram) per pound of body weight per day is considered sufficient by the Food and Nutrition Board of the U.S. National Academy of Sciences. Simply multiply your body weight by this figure to find out how much protein you should eat. Teenagers, pregnant and lactating women, children, and babies require a much higher proportion of protein in their diets, two to three times the adult minimum. For a more detailed discussion of nutritional requirements, consult one of the references listed on page 140.

How much protein food should you plan to eat each day? Calculating the amount to take isn't difficult. The chart on page 16 gives the protein content in grams for some foods that you'd commonly take hiking. You might at first try calculating the protein content of some of your hiking meals as you draw up menu plans. After you develop some familiarity with protein values, you'll be able to estimate easily the protein in a given dish.

Suppose that you at 120 pounds and a companion weighing 150 pounds are planning a trip. You will need 1.8 oz. protein per day (120 x .015 oz.), and your companion will need 2.25 oz. per day (150 x .015 oz.), for a combined total of about 4 oz. (about 114 grams) every day for the two of you.

A sample day's food might include:

	GRAMS PROTEIN
Breakfast:	
1 cup dry skim milk used on cereal and in hot chocolate	10
3 oz. oatmeal (dry weight)	12
Lunch:	
2 oz. jerky	28
4 oz. peanuts	30
Dinner:	
One-pot meal made with 4 oz. fresh cheddar cheese and 4 oz. whole-wheat macaroni	44
Total	124

You can see that it is not difficult to include enough protein in hiking menus. A generous amount of milk or cheese daily, supplemented by dried egg and a small amount of meat, is all you need. It's even easier to get plenty of protein if you make extensive use of the relatively high-protein carbohydrate foods listed in the chart when you bake goodies for the trip. Just be sure to add milk or egg to supply the amino acids lacking in these vegetable foods.

Fats are a concentrated source of energy for hikers and climbers, supplying almost twice the calories as the same weight of protein or carbohydrates. However, your stomach requires much more time to digest fats than it does to digest carbohydrates. Eaten with dinner, fats make it less likely that you'll wake up starving before dawn, but the same indulgence before you start a strenuous hike or climb may make you feel very uncomfortable. Fatty foods eaten in large quantities at any one time are likely to give you indigestion, especially at high altitudes where it is more difficult to digest them.

The least expensive, most versatile source of fat is a container of margarine tucked in your pack and spread on bread, or added to hot dishes. Other less-concentrated sources of fat like chocolate, cheese, nuts, sardines or tuna, and dry sausages are standard hikers' fare. Some fatty foods, like butter, grow rancid quickly in hot weather, and all tend to melt in heat. Keeping them cool in camp and carrying them below the hottest surface areas of your pack are good precautions.

Vitamins and minerals are necessary in your trail diet to enable your body to make the best use of your food. If you select, as we suggest, a trail diet of whole grain or enriched products, nuts, milk, cheese, eggs, and some lean meats, you will be assured of ample vitamins and minerals for body health, with the exception of vitamin C and, for women, iron.

Vitamin C is available in many soft-drink mixes and fruit juice mixes which most hikers use. Iron tablets should be taken in amounts recommended by your doctor. If you're uncertain about the ability of your trail diet to give your body enough vitamins and minerals, take daily vitamin supplements to ease your mind.

PROTEIN CONTENT OF STANDARD BACKPACKING FOODS

GRAMS OF PROTEIN IN ONE OUNCE (28 GRAMS)	FOOD
10	Dry skim milk (about 1 cup)
7	Dry whole milk
14	Dry whole eggs
11 (est.)	Dry cheddar cheese powder (¼ cup)
10	Aged parmesan or dry Monterey Jack cheese
8	Natural Swiss cheese
7	Natural cheddar cheese
9-10 (est.)	Jerky
8-9 (est.)	Wilson's meat or bacon bar
20 (est.)	Freeze-dried cooked beef or chicken chunks
7	Drained canned tuna, canned roast or corned beef, dry salami or cervelat sausage
6	Canned sardines with liquid, kippers, rainbow trout, canned chicken
5.5	Canned tongue
3-3.5	Potted meat spreads, Vienna sausage, liver paste, pate

The vegetable proteins below all lack one or more essential amino acids. In order to get the full protein value listed, eat these along with an animal food.

14 (est.)	Soybean derivative meats (TSP)
8	Pumpkin and squash seeds
7.5	Wheat germ, plain
7.3	Peanuts with skin
7	Sunflower seeds, hulled
10 (est.)	Soybeans, roasted and salted
4	Oatmeal, dry
3.5-4	Enriched or whole wheat macaroni or noodles
3	Farina
2.5-3	Whole grain or enriched breads, bulgur wheat
2	Rice: parboiled enriched, brown, or instant

WATER AND SALT

Water and salt go together in our bodies, a yin-yang pair we inherit from our ancient ocean home. The profuse sweating which comes with strenuous hiking, climbing, or skiing takes both water and salt from your body. If you are vigorously active for more than a couple of hours a day only on weekend or occasional week-long trips, you'll want to take care to replace water and salt lost. People for whom several hours of exertion is a daily thing need to worry about this less than most of us, as their bodies have adjusted to conserve salt, and they have probably learned through experience just how much they need to drink.

Most of us have experienced some discomforts of dehydration on hot hikes where water was scarce: a "cotton-mouthed" feeling, perhaps a headache, and even feelings of dizziness or weakness. Ideally, water and salt would be replaced regularly throughout any period of heavy sweating to minimize potential dehydration problems. Drinking deeply from every stream and snacking on salty food is the simplest precaution in areas where water is freely available.

On some trips, though, and on most long climbs, not enough water is available to prevent considerable dehydration. When the heat is great, and so is your exertion, 4-5 hours of profuse sweating can easily take 4-5 quarts and a proportionate amount of salt from your body. You probably develop a bad headache, feel rather weak, and may have muscle cramps. It's impossible to rehydrate quickly at the end of such a tough day, and even salty food won't replace all the salt you've lost. Keep a full water container handy and keep drinking steadily all evening, taking 2-4 salt tablets for each quart of water drunk. Put a full container nearby when you go to bed. If you don't restore the water and salt lost, you'll probably be below par the next day.

Salt tablets are useful in circumstances when you need to replace large amounts of salt lost through sweating, but can't eat enough salty food to make up the loss. Just be sure to drink generously when taking in salt tablets or salty food, and vice versa. One can't do its work without the other. Two types of salt tablets are available: regular and wax-impregnated, which are said to cause less discomfort to sensitive stomachs.

IS IT SAFE TO DRINK?

In general, the closer you are to civilization, the more important this question becomes. Bacterial contamination is likely in any residential or agricultural area, along with periodic contamination from pesticides and excess fertilizers. Some heavily-used lakes and streams far from civilization have been contaminated with bacteria through human carelessness, so that even in the "wilderness" you will want to check on water quality. For reliable information, ask the ranger who issues your fire permit, or consult recent guidebooks for the area.

The standard methods of purifying water contaminated by bacteria are (1) boiling for at least five minutes, or (2) adding halazone or iodine tablets and waiting for the chemicals to act—about thirty minutes. Air mixed into boiled water will alleviate its "flat" taste, and the tablets' chemical taste can be somewhat masked by drink mixes.

Desert hikers will want to avoid waterholes whose water contains dissolved minerals in poisonous amounts. Checking on waterholes before you start a desert trip is especially important.

SOME

SAMPLE

MENU PLANS

*Simplicity, simplicity, simplicity! I say, let
your affairs be as two or three, and not a
hundred or a thousand.*
—Henry Thoreau, *Walden*

The length of a trip is naturally the first thing to consider
in planning a menu. Short, overnight trips usually mean that
you can comfortably carry heavier or bulkier foods, but you
may want foods that cook fast. Steak and wine, for instance,
can ride fairly easily in a pack on an overnight trip. Sure,
they'll feel a lot heavier at 9,000 feet than they did at home,
but they are within the range of possibility. Careful planning
and the use of very light weight foods pays the biggest divi-
dends on longer trips where weight, storage properties, and
bulk are very important.

Plans for meals go right along with the general plans for
any outing—like them, they'll be carefully made, yet flexible.
Backpacking trips rarely go according to even the best made
plans. Weather, trail conditions, unexpected fatigue, or
unplanned-for bursts of energy often cause replanning en
route. Menu plans are best developed with a specific schedule
in mind, but once you've left the trailhead, "Dinner No. 3"
can just as well be cooked on the second night and the "lazy
breakfast" eaten on that morning you planned a quick getaway—but the fish began to bite. Planning assures you of a
meal for each mealtime on your trip. It also assures you of a

variety of foods, and if you've checked the nutrition section, a balance of essential nutrients.

A MILD-WEATHER FIVE-DAY EXPLORATION TRIP MENU

Imagine that you and three friends plan to take a five-day hike exploring a mountain Primitive Area and you have agreed to plan the food.

Looking over the maps very carefully, you choose a tentative route. The first day and the last will be spent covering ground quickly, over a known trail, in order to span the distance from the roadhead parking area to the boundary of the Primitive Area. The first night's campsite will be at a lake near the trail. Beyond this lake no one in the party knows firsthand what the terrain will be like.

The exploring days, two and four, will be spent cross-country hiking finding routes to and from the destination— a large, but apparently seldom-visited lake. Although there may be no formal trails here, you are reasonably confident that by the second night you'll be camped at the lake and that day three will be a lazy lay-over. If the going is slower than you envision, part of the third day may be spent in strenuous hiking, too.

A menu for this trip needs to be flexible, contain plenty of calories, and offer a variety of possibilities. As you read through the recipe titles, keep in mind that Chicken Curry could become Fish Curry if you've caught a lot of fish, that Wholewheat Pancakes served with Gorp Syrup make a grand dessert . . .

BREAKFAST: five days, four servings each day
Day 1—a fast start from the roadside parking area
      Granola
      Dried, or fresh, milk (fresh milk in a vacuum bottle)
      Freeze-dried coffee
Day 2—full power start for a long day
      Real Oatmeal with Breakfast Gorp, dried milk
      Hiker's Cocoa I or II
Day 3—lay-over day, lazy breakfast
      Wholewheat Pancakes with Breakfast Gorp Syrup
      Bacon, bacon bar, or bacon bits (soy)
      Freeze-dried coffee
Day 4—back on the trail again for a long day
      Mushroom Omelet
      Honey-Banana Bread
      Hiker's Cocoa I or II
Day 5—going out, a fast getaway
      Familia, dried milk
      Hiker's Cocoa, or freeze-dried coffee

Note: Add a serving of fruit juice crystals to these breakfasts if you wish. Although it's not mentioned, margarine is added to the oatmeal, pancakes, and omelet, so plan on two or three additional tablespoons for each of these meals when you make up the general supply of margarine.

LUNCHES
Midday eating can be a time when each hiker has his druthers —some enjoy eating only when they can take off their packs and sit down, while others will nibble happily, step after step,

down the trail. If each member of a party carries his own "nose-bag," handy in an outside pack pocket, he can dip into it often, or reserve it for a break, as he chooses. Further, no one is ever in the uncomfortable and potentially dangerous position of being without quick-energy food if he becomes separated from the rest of the party.

Individual lunch bags can be filled with a variety of gorps, cheeses, salami, jerky, trail breads, and so forth. Each member is usually responsible for making up his own bag from the general supply (page 23). Each member is also responsible for making his supply last for the duration of the trip.

As a matter of convenience, however, beverages and soups are shared in common by all. Usually, a pot of soup, or a quart of fruit drink, is part of the longest midday break. A second break may be important to parties that include children or less-experienced hikers. For everyone, breaks help fend off fatigue.

On this trip, plan from five to ten group portions, depending on whether you think you'll need one, or two, midday breaks.

Use commercial fruit drink mixes, soup mixes, milkshake mixes. These mixes are most easily carried by the person with the potset.

DINNERS: five days, four servings each
Day 1—getting back into trail routines
    Spicy Tomato Soup
    Cheese and Rice Plus
    Honest-to-Chocolate Pudding
    Coffee, tea, or cocoa
Day 2—covering many miles, time to eat heartily
    Bloody Harry cocktail
    Hyatt Lake Goulash
    Date Cake
    Coffee, tea, or cocoa
Day 3—the lay-over day, maybe some fresh fish, too
    (The fresh fish may be cooked your favorite way and

served as a first course, or used as a substitute for the chicken in Chicken Curry.)
Chicken Curry
Apple Crisp
Coffee, tea, or cocoa
Day 4—another long day
Lemon-Lime Swizzle with Garlic Crunch
Spaghetti and Meatballs
Apricot Smash
Coffee, tea, or cocoa
Day 5—waiting in the car at the trailhead
Chicken Ala King (canned, 2 cans)
Rice (instant)
Your favorite canned fruit plus other special favorites, such as date-nut bread, smoked clams, lobster bisque
The usual drinks

GENERAL ADDITIONAL SUPPLIES
Margarine, 2 pounds or more (an easily varied item, more of it provides more calories for more strenuous trips)
Sugar and powdered coffee creamer, if you use them
Extra servings of Hiker's Cocoa (also provides added calories and energy in a pinch)
Flour, or cornmeal, if you use it for frying fish
Packets of lemon crystals for seasoning fish
Salt and pepper

ELEMENTS OF A NO-COOK TRIP MENU
There may be a particular trip, or several days within a longer trip, when you feel it's wise to trim weight, fuel, and food-preparation time to an absolute minimum. Perhaps part of your route involves a long steep climb, or possibly you plan a tour cross-country skiing. In either case, high-energy foods will definitely be needed, but some will be ready to eat without cooking while others may need only the addition of hot water.

In this last group you'll think first of soup mixes and hot drinks. This is the time to load the Hiker's Cocoa with whole dried milk for extra fat calories, for example.

Many foods you'll eat just as they come from your pack. This list will suggest some of the possibilities:

Semi-sweet chocolate, the old stand-by

Granola and familia

Homemade milkshake mixes loaded with extra dried milk

Beef jerky, salami, commercial meatbar, and baconbar

Liver sausage, blood sausage

Mincemeat bars

Any of the trail breads—whole-wheat, Logan, and so forth

Dried, yet semi-moist, fruits—apricots, prunes, etc.

Nuts, peanut butter, lots of margarine

In *The Complete Walker,* a backpacking classic, Colin Fletcher has many further suggestions for foods that involve little or no cooking. As you thumb through our recipe section, you'll see a number of other items that would make good fare on a no-cook trip.

GETTING IT
ALL TOGETHER

Let us not be upset and overwhelmed in that
terrible rapid whirlpool called a dinner . . .
Weather this danger and you are safe, for the
rest of the way is down hill.
— Henry Thoreau, *Walden*

Repacking and prepackaging food items at home simplifies
trail cooking and cuts down on meal preparation time when
it really counts—when YOU are tired and hungry.

A table, the cleared-off kitchen counter, even the floor,
can serve as a staging area for the pack-up operation. It's
handy to have a household scale that will measure up to ten
pounds, but if you don't, you can use a regular measuring
cup for doling out measured quantities of food. A small notebook and a pencil are invaluable aids. Record the quantities
of food you take on each trip, then don't forget to take the
notebook along. Every few meals, at least, note what things
you wish there'd been more of, or less, as well as preferences
and dislikes. You'll forget quickly otherwise.

Labeling as you pack helps avoid identity crises in camp.
A sheet of stick-on labels or a roll of masking tape and a
marking pen are all you need.

Finally, the food items are all gathered together in some
open work area, there's a scale or cup handy, the notebook
lies open, and the labels are waiting to be written on, but
something is missing.

What are you going to get it together *in?*

BAGS AND OTHER CONTAINERS

Bags offer a sound combination of economy, convenience, minimum weight and bulk, and reusability, but they don't meet absolutely every backpacking need. For example, freeze-dried products are often packaged in their own foil packets. Don't repackage them. These pouches are moisture tight and will serve as good containers for rehydrating the food. Some other items like commercial soup mixes and fruit drinks also come in foil packets, and are best left unopened as they tend to pick up moisture and form hard lumps if not tightly sealed. Along with this moisture pick-up goes some loss of flavor, too. Sometimes you can wash out these tough foil packets and use them again. They are particularly good for repacking tomato crystals from a bulk supply. Tomato crystals are probably the most hygroscopic food backpackers carry and go from light flakes to rocky lumps quickly when exposed to moist air.

Most of the other food items you'll be carrying can be repackaged in plastic or cloth bags. Bags are soft and flexible. They nestle into the corners and squeeze into the crannies of a backpack. When they're empty, fold them flat for the trip home.

The heavy, freezer-type, gallon-size plastic bags are good for packing large quantities of a single food, or complete meals. They close securely with wire twist-ties. The small, thin plastic sandwich bags are handy for separating small bits of stuff within a heavy bag, but don't use them alone. They are fragile and will leak.

Heavy plastic bags can be washed and reused several times, but you'll get the maximum in reusability if you make your own bags. These custom-sewn bags will travel with you year after year ... after year.

Buy remnants of lightweight coated nylon fabric or a medium-weight vinyl (sources page 141).

HOW TO MAKE A FOOD BAG

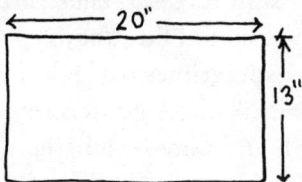

1. Cut a rectangle 20"x13". If you are using coated nylon stitch coated side in. Nylon may be hot cut with a soldering iron, this will prevent seams from raveling.

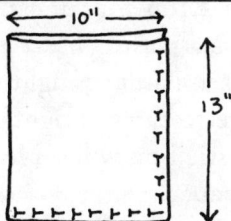

2. Fold in half. Pin cut edges together on two sides. Leave a 10" edge open. This will be top of bag.

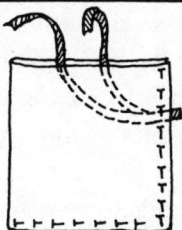

3. Cut a 20" length of twill tape. Fold it in half and pin about 3" from the top and between the two 13" edges.

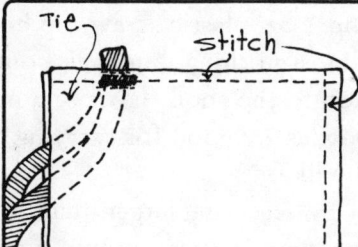

4. Stitch the pinned edges together about ¼" from the edge. Stitch several times over the place where tie is caught in the seam.

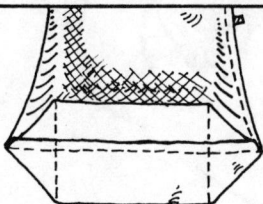

Tie

stitch

5. To make box bottom fold the bottom seam against the side seam and stitch across the corner.

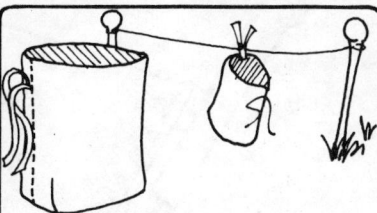

6. Turn the bag right side out. The bag will sit upright and open. These bags may be machine washed on a warm cycle + drip dried.

Margarine is one food that doesn't travel in bags. Traditionally backpackers have carried margarine in aluminum screw top containers called "provision boxes." These boxes have a plastic insert and a double-gasketed lid. Yet even with this apparently tight closure, they sometimes do leak. Be sure to carry it right-side-up in your pack. A good screw-top plastic box will serve about as well and may be a little cheaper.

Raw eggs do pack safely in preformed plastic egg boxes. These hinged boxes are available in two, four, and six egg sizes. As you'll notice, our recipes depend on whole dried eggs and they can be bagged, confidently.

Some of our recipes do call for small amounts of liquid flavoring. It's easy to carry such flavorings in ¼ oz., ½ oz., and 1 oz. plastic screw-top bottles. These tiny vials weigh almost nothing, but their contents can make a big contribution to the good flavor of a meal. Empty film cans and pill bottles are good for carrying tiny amounts of dry spices and the like.

For carrying larger quantities of liquids, other than water, there are spun aluminum pint and quart bottles with rubber-gasketed screw tops. Although you may carry one of these full of stove fuel, another could be filled with rum, brandy, vodka, or whatever you prefer.

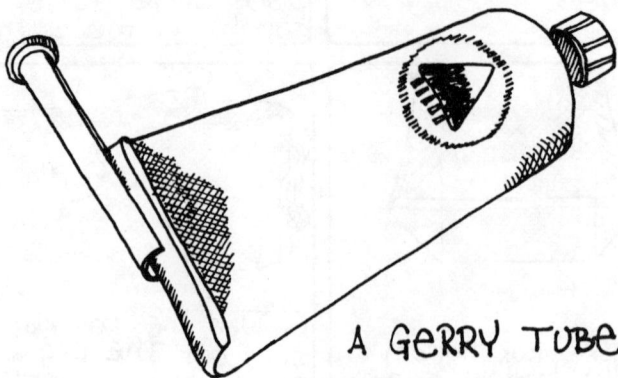

A GERRY TUBE

Mountain shops and mail order outlets carry a variety of these bottles and boxes designed to meet some of the carrying requirements of particular foods. They also usually sell Gerry tubes, a variation on traditional packing containers. The Gerry tube looks something like a large plastic toothpaste tube with one end cut off. This open end lets you fill the tube easily with jam, honey, peanut butter, mustard, or any other similar material. Then, you fold over the open end and secure it with a special plastic clip. To use the contents, unscrew the cap on the other end and squeeze, carefully.

Many of the foods described in this sample menu plan could be carried in screw-top plastic containers instead of bags, if you prefer. Plastic containers abound in the variety stores, the supermarkets, and probably in your own kitchen. If you do go the plastic container route, be sure the ones you use can be easily and thoroughly cleaned, even boiled, between trips. Plastic tends to absorb flavors, odors, and oils from the contents. Sometimes these oils foster the growth of bacteria, which in turn could be the culprit in a stomach upset on the next outing.

So, gather up the bags, special bottles, plastic containers, and whatever else looks promising. You are now ready to pack up.

PACKING UP
Now, let's imagine that you're packing up the sample menu from pages 21, 22, and 23. Where do you begin?

1. At the beginning—BREAKFASTS. Look down the list. *Which items appear just once?* Measure and bag each of these in a separate bag. You'll have granola, oatmeal, whole-wheat pancake mix, bacon bits, and familia. Stick a label on each bag noting what's inside and how much water to add, if water is to be added. Now look again. *Which items appear twice?* Measure and bag two days' servings in one bag. Now note *items that contain several ingredients.* In this menu, it's

Mushroom Omelet. Follow the recipe directions for bagging and labeling. Are there *foods that will be used many meals?* Label large bags for cocoa, dry milk, and items like these that will be used again and again. Got everything? The Honey-Banana Bread should still be there on your table. It will need to be wrapped tightly in plastic wrap or foil.

2. LUNCHES—using the individual lunch bag plan. Label one heavy plastic or cloth bag with the name of each hiker. Let each person fill his own bag from the assortment of gorp, cheese, chocolate, and so forth. If there is danger of a favorite food not being equally shared, you may want to divide it in equal portions in advance. Remember that these bags will represent a little less than a third of each day's food, and for a five-day trip will weigh from 2½ to 3½ pounds. Shared lunch items are simply gathered into one or two big bags. These include the soup mixes, fruit drinks, and milkshakes.

3. DINNERS. Label four of the large size bags as No. 1, No. 2, No. 3, and No. 4. Dinner No. 5 can be packed in a grocery sack and left in the car. Check each item of Dinner No. 1. Measure and bag according to the directions in the recipe section. Be sure to mark bags with the quantity of water to be added, or put this information in your notebook. Put all the smaller bags into the large one and close it with a twist tie. Dinner No. 1 for this trip is now all in one place, ready to go when you hit camp. Get the others together in the same way.

When all the food has been bagged, weigh the total. Don't forget to include the general supplies listed on page 23. There should be 1½ to 2 pounds of dried or freeze-dried foods for each person, each day.

If your food total varies much from this rule of thumb, look again at what you are taking. Have you chosen dried or dehydrated foods whenever possible? What are the heaviest items you are taking? Could you substitute something lighter? Or, if your total is considerably below this figure, look again at the portions you've allowed. Are they realistic? It may be wise to add a little extra.

BREAKFASTS

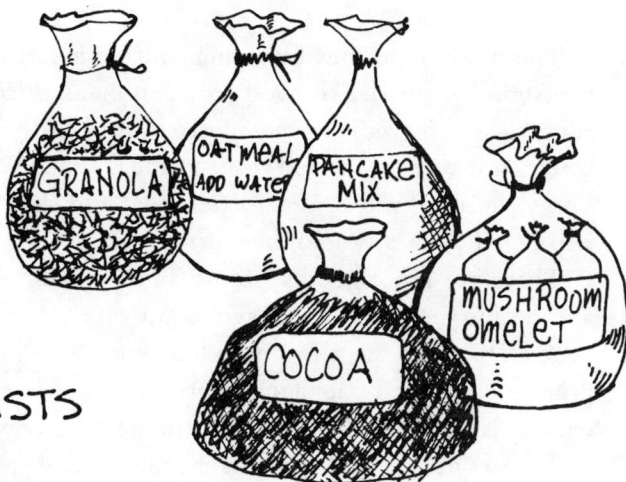

LUNCHES

DINNERS

The pre-trip per-meal bagging routine insures you of premeasured quantities of food for each meal. With this system each bagged ingredient is ready to add to hot water, or have water, hot or cold, added to it, at meal time. You always know there is food for each trail meal and that preparation will be easy for any member of the party.

There are other good systems for apportioning trail meals and with experience you'll work out one that fits your own needs. However, we think you'll eventually wind up with a premeasuring and packaging method somewhat like the one we've just described. Savings of time and energy on the trail, and the control you'll have over menu quality, make the effort worthwhile.

As you stuff food bags into the packs, stuff in a couple of extra large plastic bags, too. Those sold as garbage can liners are good for all sorts of situations. One such bag split open will provide a rain cover for your pack, or two worn inside your boots, outside your socks, can keep your feet dry in unexpectedly wet weather. They are also ideal for packing out litter and trash. It's no longer enough just to pack out what you brought in. If the wilderness is to survive, every hiker must pack out as much litter and trash as he can carry. The buck stops with you, and with me.

COOKING
GEAR

It was pleasant to see my whole household
effects out on the grass, making a little pile
...so much more interesting most familiar
objects look out of doors than in the house.
—Henry Thoreau, *Walden*

The basic equipment needed to prepare meals for from two
to four hikers will probably tip the scales at from two to five
pounds, and each ounce of those pounds may be carried
over many miles of trail. The choice of each ounce obviously
is very important.

STOVES AND FUELS
Although many backpackers still use wood fires for cooking,
the trend is toward the use of stoves, particularly in wood-
poor and ecologically sensitive areas. Here's why.

1. Stoves don't leave ugly fire scars.
2. Stoves needn't damage fragile plant life.
3. Stoves provide reliable heat. In some heavily camped
places there simply isn't any firewood left.
4. Stoves can be turned off. They won't leave glowing
coals to spark a forest fire.

In some areas of the West, open fires have been restricted
because of fire danger, or the need for preserving a sensitive
environment. As more urban vacationers look for recreation
experiences in the woods and mountains, restrictions on

open fires are likely to increase. Respecting these ordinances can help preserve the beauty of forests and mountains for the many hiking seasons and generations yet to come.

Which stove to choose? Backpacking stoves are of three types. Each kind burns a different fuel—white gas, kerosene, or liquid butane. Each has its conveniences and its drawbacks.

A WHITE GAS STOVE (SVEA 123) & A FUEL BOTTLE

White gas stoves are probably the most commonly used by backpackers. These stoves need no special priming fuel. If you are reasonably warm-blooded, you simply cup your hands around the fuel tank. The warmth of your hands forces a little of the gas into the burner, from whence it trickles down into a priming cup. If your hands aren't that warm, try holding a lighted match under the bottom of the fuel tank for a minute or two. Once a little gas is in the cup, strike a match and ignite it. The heat resulting both (a) creates pressure which forces fuel into the burner, and (b) vaporizes it.

This stove once lit doesn't need any further pumping. It is regulated by a sometimes pesky valve between tank and burner. White gas is readily available at discount stores and some service stations for about 80 cents a gallon.

White gas stoves must never be filled while they're hot—this fuel does explode. As a matter of routine, fill your stove at the start of each meal's preparation when the stove is cold. It's also a good idea to use a small filter funnel to keep dirt particles from clogging the fuel line.

The smallest of these stoves is the Svea 123. There is an Optimus 80/Primus 21L that is a little bigger and folds into its own box. There are larger models that operate in the same way, but which are designed to hold more fuel and have stronger pot supports for preparing meals for larger parties.

Kerosene stoves use a less volatile fuel, and for this reason are somewhat safer. But it does take the heat of an alcohol flame and some skill to get them started. The first step is to pour a little alcohol into the primer cup under the burner. This alcohol is ignited with a match, and, unless the wind is high, it will heat the tube and burner enough to vaporize kerosene. When the alcohol is almost burned out, a couple of strokes on the air pump pushes fuel up into the burner—kerosene does not create its own pressure in the tank, as white gas does. This fuel should appear as a white vapor, *not* a liquid. If liquid kerosene squirts up, the preheating hasn't worked. Once the burner is started, a few more strokes on the pump bring the stove to full output. Under full pressure, larger kerosene stoves will put out heat faster than gasoline models, an advantage under some conditions—but give the burner a minute or two to get to a high temperature before you pump too hard. You get the stove from blowtorch mode back to simmer by letting off pressure via a small valve atop the filler cap.

Kerosene is sold at hardware stores and some service stations for about the same price as white gas. Be sure and buy only clean fresh kerosene, as filtering will not reclaim gummy fuel. If your stove repeatedly clogs, and you can't see any dirt in the fuel, use that kerosene for cleaning paint brushes and start again with a fresh gallon.

The smallest kerosene stove is the Optimus/Primus 96L and it is about 8 ounces heavier than the smallest white gas models. However, this stove is made of a heavier brass stock and offers good stability for heavier pots. Several larger models are also available, with wind-resistant "roarer" burners or silent burners.

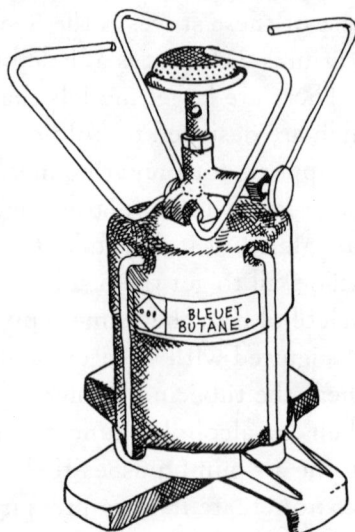

A CARTRIDGE STOVE

The *butane cartridge* stove is the easiest to operate. No priming or pumping is needed. You simply attach the cartridge, turn the valve, light the burner, and cook. Once the cartridge is in place, you must leave it there and keep the stove assembled until the cartridge is empty. This makes a bulky object to show in your pack. Probably the most serious objection to this stove is the cost of the fuel—each cartridge costs about 90 cents and is expected to give about three hours heat. The cartridges, like tin cans, need to be packed out when empty. They aren't refillable either. Some outfitters do offer a 5 cent refund on returned empty cartridges.

The most widely seen of these stoves is the Bleuet, weighing in somewhere between the Svea 123 and the smallest Primus. Friends who've used them tell us that they are slow in putting out heat. They plan a little extra time for meal preparation.

Tin fuel flasks or spun aluminum fuel bottles are a necessity for either the white gas stoves or the kerosene models on all but short trips. Both types come with snug sealing gaskets to prevent untimely fuel leaks, but remember to look at the gaskets from time to time and when they look tired, replace them.

Matches are vital to the operation of all stoves. Wooden kitchen matches, the strike-anywhere variety, are best. A match case keeps them both dry and handy.

A flint stick, or sparker, is also good for lighting some stoves. It operates like a cigarette lighter without the fluid. This tiny spark is often enough to light vaporized kerosene, and flints last almost indefinitely. Be sure to check the flint for the sparker, though, and refill match cases between outings.

POTS, CUPS, AND CUTLERY

Cooking gear needs to be very light. That's why most pots made for backpacking are aluminum. You'll need at least two pots, one nesting inside the other. They'll either have handles that fold down, or no handles at all, but they will have lids. It's ideal when one lid can also be a frypan.

Among the pots found at most mountaineering shops, there are three major styles. There are *billies*—straight-sided pots modeled after the old tin can with a wire handle that folds down. These are made in many sizes, as are *kettles*— shallower pots, often spun aluminum, with rounded bottoms and wide bail handles that also fold down or lock in the upright position. *Cooksets* usually consist of two nesting pots of stamped aluminum, with folding or detached handles, and a lid/frypan of some sort. One typical cookset has a 2-quart and a 3-quart pot with lids and a teflon coated frypan. It nests together neatly and will provide enough cooking equipment for four hikers. Another slightly different cookset is the one designed to fit the Svea 123 stove (page 35). This set nests neatly, has lid/fry pan, and the two pots also stack to make a double boiler. The kit includes an extra wind-screen device, to boot.

NESTING BILLIES

But backpacking pots need not come from mountaineering shops, nor have started life as backpacking equipment. Very adequate pots can be converted, or modified, from resale shop, variety store, or your own kitchen models.

First, find two straight-sided aluminum pans that will nest and do have lids. The next step is to make them handleless. Some people simply use a hacksaw and saw off any existing handle. Others drill out the rivets that hold the handle on by using a ¼-inch electric drill, and then plug the holes with new aluminum rivets from the hardware store. Detached handles are made by Sigg, and others, and are called "pot lifters." The pot lifter will clamp on the side of these now-handleless pans. The same process converts a small frypan into a handle-less backpacker's skillet.

A very valuable part of the pot set, although it's hard to find ready-made, is the *pot bag*. It's usually made of ripstop nylon and has a round bottom that just fits the larger pot. The top is secured with a drawstring and a drawstring clamp. It will keep any sootiness on the pots and off the inside of your pack, and also keeps whatever else you carry inside those pots neatly inside.

38

The space inside the pots offers ideal storage for some of the other small things you'll use at mealtimes. Among these are *cups*. Although it may seem awkward till you've tried it, cups make a good all-purpose dish. They can be used not only for drinking, but take the place of a bowl and plate as well.

The stainless steel cup, often called the Sierra cup, has been a favorite of backpackers for several generations. It has a wire handle that doesn't get hot, making it easy to handle a cup full of hot soup or cocoa, and it rinses clean with a small swish of water. Another popular cup is a plastic one that clips to the belt and is two ounces lighter than the Sierra cup. Soot and grease do seem to cling to it, though.

Two-ounce aluminum plates offer another very light dish. Unfortunately, aluminum bleeds the heat from food very quickly and if you choose these, your dinner may be cold as you take the first bite.

To complement the simplicity of using just one cup for everything, try using just one wide-bowled spoon, too. There are some very light weight ones available, with short handles that fit easily into pot sets or pack pockets. A spoon from your regular supply (inexpensive stainless steel, probably) can be modified to serve as well by shortening its handle with a hacksaw. The short handle cuts the over-all weight of the spoon and makes it easier to pack.

Dishwashing supplies can hide inside the pot set, too. A small plastic bottle filled with liquid biodegradable soap and a stainless steel pot scrubber are all you need, although a piece of linen dish towel is handy sometimes. If you sew small loops on one edge of that towel, it can hang out to dry from a pack-tie between meals.

HOW TO MAKE A POT BAG
MAKING THE PATTERN

+ 2"

1. measure pot at widest point + add two inches.

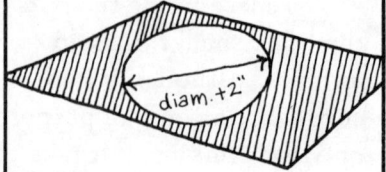

diam.+2"

2. measure and cut circle pattern from a newspaper.

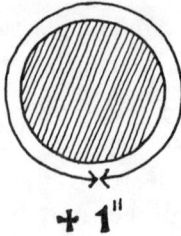

+ 1"

3. To make rectangle, measure around the perimeter of pattern circle + add one inch. This is length of rectangle.

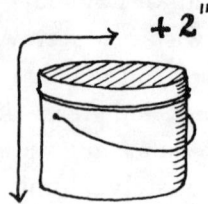

+ 2"

4. measure height of cook set with lid on plus ½ diam. of circle pattern plus 2". this is height of rectangle. Cut rectangle from newspaper.

HOW TO MAKE A POT BAG
SEWING THE BAG

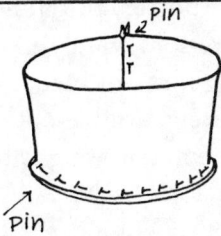

1. With right sides together pin the long edge of the rectangle to the bottom circle. Adjust rectangle to fit bottom. Allow ½" for bottom seam.

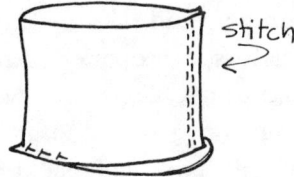

2. Stitch side seam from top to bottom. Stitch again ¼" from first seam. Trim with pinking shears.

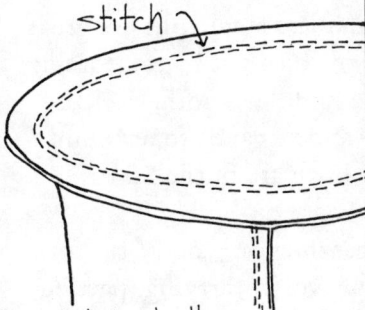

3. Stitch bottom to rectangle - stitch twice.

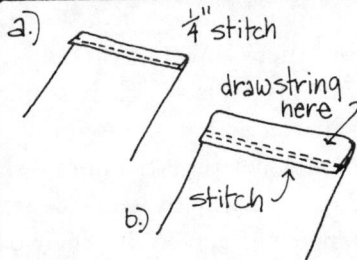

4. To form drawstring tunnel a) Roll + stitch ¼" edge around top of bag. b) Roll + stitch another seam ¾" from top. Leave 1" for drawstring.

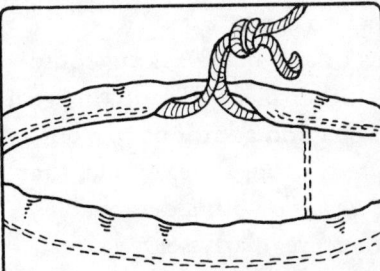

5. Cut a length of Nylon cord. Burn ends w/ flame. Run cord through tunnel. Install a drawstring clamp or tie ends together.

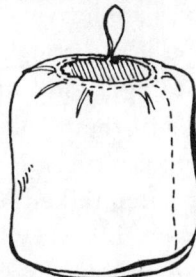

6. Finished bag looks like this.

SOME MORE USEFUL ITEMS

One sharp knife. You'll need it for hacking off chunks of
salami, cleaning fish, spreading peanut butter, and hundreds
of other jobs. "Swiss Army" knives are sold widely to
campers and they feature an intriguing array of blades—
scissors, can openers, a reamer, corkscrew, double-cut saw,
and so on. There are several models ranging in weight from
one to five ounces. But for most situations a simple, lightweight, two-blade jackknife is sufficient. On longer trips,
you can tuck a small whetstone into your pack to keep it
sharp.

A salt and pepper container. Look for one that holds both,
has shaker tops on either end, and can be completely sealed
with screw-top lids.

A backpacking grill. For times when wood fires are legal,
and there is wood, these light stainless steel grills are great.
One model is a slightly squared-off oval with a reinforcing
bar welded lengthwise down the middle. Another one is
modeled after a trombone slide and expands to accommodate a variety of fireplace sizes. Both are in the $5 to $7
range and come with their own bags.

A folding saw. If you are depending on wood fires for
cooking, a Sven-style saw may be worth carrying, particularly in well-timbered areas or on canoe trips. With it,
downed timber can be converted quickly into fireplace fuel
and bridges built to make safe crossings of flooded streams.
Hand axes are heavier and bulkier to carry.

As you leaf through the pages of any backpacking equipment catalogs, you'll spot many other pieces of cooking gear
and some of them will prove to be good additions to your
kit. There is a tiny, lightweight *tea kettle,* for example, that
we have often talked of buying. A *ladle* with a detachable
handle would be very helpful if you regularly serve larger
groups. A tiny folding *can opener* may be needed, and on
and on.

As you look around the kitchen you'll spot useful utensils

that can be modified for trail use, too. The ubiquitous *rubber scraper,* or spatula, with its handle sawed short, makes a very good pot stirrer and pancake turner, besides still functioning as a rubber scraper. The gravy blender becomes a *chain shaker* with the addition of three or four inches of chain from the hardware store. This shaker will provide lumpless blending while also serving as a standard measuring cup, a ladle, and an extra drinking cup.

There are other convenience or luxury items, if you want to carry their added weight. One is the *reflector oven.* Folded, it is only a little more than a foot square by about one inch deep, but it does add 2½ pounds to your pack.

When it is vital to conserve stove fuel on a long hike at high altitudes, the lightweight *pressure cooker* is a well-justified addition to the gear. To be sure, it's rather heavy, three pounds, but it cuts the cooking time of many foods significantly—brown rice, for example. For winter camping when days are short, a *candle lantern* provides steady light to cook by.

One more basic item belongs with the cooking gear—a 25-foot length of 550-pound test *nylon pack-hanging cord.* Pack hanging only takes a few minutes, easily becomes a part of the regular routine, and can help you avoid food-seeking animals.

To hang a pack, first find a tree and select a limb about 15 feet off the ground. Then, tie a rock about the size of your fist on one end of the cord and toss rock/rope over the limb. Tie the free end of cord to your pack and haul the pack up to the limb. Tie the free end securely to whatever is handy. Hung in this way your pack and its contents will be safe from all but the most acrobatic bears and low-flying squirrels. If you are camped in a place where there are no trees, the chances are there are also very few animals.

By the way, bears aren't the only pack thieves in the woods. All members of the mouse, chipmunk, and squirrel clans love to eat people food, too, and can make a real mess of your pack if you leave it on the ground. Zipping all the pack zippers and tying down the flaps very securely will keep these tiny robbers out. Carrying only non-fragrant dried and freeze-dried foods also makes your pack less attractive to wildlife.

SETTING UP

A TRAIL KITCHEN

My house was on the side of a hill, immediately on the edge of the larger wood, in the midst of a young forest of pitch pines and hickories, and a half a dozen rods from the pond...
    —Henry Thoreau, *Walden*

Stop and look around for a minute or two after you've decided to camp for the night. Take that time to find the most comfortable and convenient spot the site affords before you set up a trail kitchen.

For a trail kitchen in which you'll use a stove, look for a place where the stove can be shielded from the wind. All backpacking stoves operate best when they are sheltered from any breeze. Sometimes they seem to sense a wind even when you don't. Stoves are easier to work with on firm ground, or rock. If the soil is soft and sandy, you may need to find some flat rocks or splinters of wood to rest the stove on. If the day is sunny and bright, try to find a patch of shade for the kitchen, for your own comfort. Sometimes the whole kitchen operation can be arranged up off the ground on a rock ledge, or a fallen tree can be found to provide counter space.

There isn't quite as much freedom of choice in locating a cooking area when you use a wood fire. In a heavily camped place, a stone fireplace will already have been built, years ago, by other campers. If the stones can be rearranged to fit your grill, use the existing fireplace. Making a new one will only leave more fire-scarred places and rocks to mar the serenity of the campsite.

If you are camping in a remote, seldom-used spot, and other campers have carefully taken apart their fireplaces—replacing the rocks with the fire scars hidden—build yours keeping in mind that you, too, will hide all the visible traces of your visit.

If you must camp in a meadow, where the ground is unscarred and covered with fragile flowers and meadow grass, do as some Indians did. Cut a small square in the turf and lift it out intact, carefully. Arrange the rocks to hold up your grill within this cut and build a small fire. When you are finished cooking and the embers are cool, remove the rocks and replace them where you found them. Then smooth out the charred bits of wood and replace the square of turf. No one will ever know you were there.

Once you have picked the spot for your stove or fire, unload the cooking gear. As a matter of routine, fill the fuel tank of a gas or kerosene stove before you light it. Then you're always sure it won't run out of fuel during a meal. Stoves must be filled ONLY when they are cold.

Setting up a wood fire means taking into account many more variables than does setting up a stove. If there is no fireplace or you are rearranging one, put one rock on either side of the fire area the right distance apart to comfortably support your grill. You may need to stack several together in order to build this grill-support up about eight inches from the ground. Plan to allow six to eight inches for the fire. Then pile more rocks along the back edge to reflect heat toward the pot. The open side of the fireplace should be oriented to catch some wind for draft.

While the fireplace is being built someone else can scrounge for wood. Use only downed or fallen trees for firewood. Breaking dead-looking branches off living trees is now illegal in most places and hard on the trees. Don't bother with wood that looks rotten, as it will not give much heat. Choose dry, white, firm pieces in an assortment of sizes.

THIS ALLOWS 8" PLENTY OF OF AIR CIRCULATION

To start the cooking fire, pick one good dry stick about two inches in diameter and lay it front to back in the fireplace. Pile against it a handful of very tiny twigs. Those the size of toothpicks are best. They heat quickly to their kindling temperature. This fire is sometimes called a "lean-to" fire. There are other good ways to arrange wood and kindling, too. For descriptions of some of them check the other books on backpacking on pages 139 and 140.

Hold one lighted wooden match under the pile of twigs, shielding it with your hands and body if the wind is high. In a moment or two the twigs will usually be blazing. Damp wood doesn't burn this readily. It must be dried out and then kindled. This is where fire starters come in handy.

Fire starters are simply small coils of corrugated paper dipped in paraffin. To make them, cut strips of corrugated paper about one inch wide and six or eight inches long. Roll up and secure with a pin or rubber band. Then melt a bar of paraffin. Remember, heat it in a can or pan, in another pan of water; never melt paraffin over direct heat. Dip the coils of paper in the liquid paraffin and arrange them on a baking rack to cool. Discard the pins, or rubber bands, when the starters are cool enough to handle. A plastic bag of these little coils weighs only a few ounces, but will provide that extra heat needed to start fires quickly when wood is damp. Some people always carry them.

Once the fire is burning steadily, add a few larger sticks. Work gradually up to sticks one or two inches in diameter. An easily controlled cooking fire can be based on two or three of these larger sticks burning well on a bed of hot coals. By simply moving these sticks together directly under the pot or easing them away, you can regulate the flow of heat to the kettle.

This cooking fire is very compact. If you plan to use a reflector oven, remove the grill, spread the coals out to about the width of the oven, and arrange fresh sticks parallel to the front of the oven.

When the evening sky seems to threaten rain or wet snow during the night, gather enough dry wood for a breakfast fire and stow it inside the tent or in one of those extra large size plastic bags. If all the wood is damp but you've managed to get a small fire going, lay a few pieces of wood around the fire to dry out. Avoid putting damp pieces directly on the fire whenever you can.

POT BOILING

Water boiling is a key technique for preparing most trail meals. Meal preparation becomes almost effortless if you practice until water boiling becomes second nature. Best of all, no one member of the party needs to do all the cooking—after all, can't everyone boil water?

The rules are simple. The first thing to do when setting up camp in the evening, or rising in the morning, is to fill the pot with water. The next is to put it on to heat. All else follows.

THE ONE-POT SYSTEM

The stove is burning, or the fire is started, and the water's on. Lay out and look over the bags for the meal.

1. If your larger pot is big enough, make sure it contains about the amount of water needed for soup, hot drinks, and presoaking of dehydrated foods as needed. *Note:* Mark the side of a pot by stamping either a line or dot into the metal at the most often used intervals—4 cups, 6 cups, and so forth. Simply measure water into the pot at home, mark where it touches the side of the pot, empty it out, hold a screwdriver blade on the mark and tap it carefully with a hammer.

2. When the water is hot, ladle out what is needed for hot drinks.
3. Add presoaking water to main dish ingredients that need it, in their foil packets, an extra cup, or whatever's handy.
4. Add a soup mix, or mixes, to the remaining water and simmer a few minutes before serving. In those minutes, relax and drink your hot beverage.
5. Serve the soup. While everyone's enjoying the soup, add cold water to the pot and put in the main dish ingredients that need the longest cooking. Any remnants of soup will enhance the main dish.
6. Continue to simmer the main dish, adding the remaining ingredients. Add more water if it seems dry, or leave the lid off it it's soupy.
7. When it's done, serve it.
8. Refill the pot and heat. This water is for more hot drinks, dessert, and/or dishwashing.

The one-pot system practically guarantees a leisurely meal-time pace. The same easy rhythm works for breakfast, too. The first hot water is used for coffee or cocoa, then the next for hot cereal, and finally more hot drinks and dishwashing. It's a simple routine—fill, heat, empty, eat; fill, heat ...

THE TWO-POT ROUTINE

For this system you'll need two cooking pots and two stoves or a fire big enough to heat both pots at once. Again, start with the bags for that meal laid out so you can see what needs to be done first.
1. Fill one pot and bring the water to a boil. Use part of this water for hot drinks and presoaking.
2. Measure water into the second pot for soup and bring it to a boil.
3. While the soup is heating, begin cooking the main dish in the first pot.

4. Eat soup and rinse the pot. Fill again with water and reheat. This water is to be used for soaking dessert fruit, more hot drinks, and/or dishwashing.
5. By now the main dish is done and can be eaten.
6. More hot drinks, dessert, and plenty of hot water for cleanup.

This system is a little speedier than the one-pot method and is probably easier whenever there is a group of more than four.

BAKING IN A TRAIL KITCHEN

Fresh-baked cakes or biscuits take very little time to prepare and add variety to hiking fare. All the recipes in this book require only the addition of water to premeasured and blended ingredients. Of course, any of the commercial cake, quick bread, or biscuit mixes that need only water can be used in the same way.

The reflector oven (page 52) makes the baking process practically foolproof. Shiny surfaces both above and below the baking shelf direct the heat from the fire toward the baking pan. The amount of heat is regulated by simply moving the oven closer or father away from the fire. For this reason it's essential to clear a space in front of the fire where the oven can stand level and be moved easily.

In our experience, this kind of oven bakes best in front of a lively fire. This means that you'll want to have a good supply of wood within easy reach and keep the fire burning about the same level throughout the baking. If the thing to be baked would be baking in a hot oven (400° F.) at home, place the oven quite close to the fire. Or, if you would ordinarily use a moderate oven (350°-375° F.), begin with the reflector oven back slightly.

During the baking process you may find it best to take the pan out and turn it around once or twice. This keeps the front half of the cake from getting done before the back half.

51

Test for doneness by piercing the cake with a long pine needle. If no batter sticks to the needle, the cake is done. When there aren't any pine needles around, touch the cake lightly in the center. If it feels springy, it's done.

A Reflector Oven

CLEANING UP

...now, a taste for the beautiful is most cultivated out of doors, where there is no house and no housekeeper.
—Henry Thoreau, Walden

Cleaning up after a trail meal is simple and fast. Either the one- or two-pot system provides you with plenty of steaming hot water when you finish eating. Use part of it diluted

to a comfortable temperature for dishwashing and the remainder for rinsing. It's really not necessary to use that biodegradable detergent more than once a day, as plain hot water is very often sufficient for a good wash job.

When you do use detergent, be sure to rinse each item completely. Soapy residues on dishes sometimes are the cause of digestive upsets.

Air dry the dishes on a clean rock, or hand dry with a towel. Remember, dishwater must be dumped at least 100 feet away from any source of water.

When you cook over a wood fire, the pots, your hands, and everything you touch will be coated with soot. The dishwater may take care of your hands, but keeping the outside of pots soot-free is another matter. You can simply drop them in their pot bags and ignore the whole thing, but each time you do handle that pot you'll come up with black fingers. A soapy water scrub with a stainless steel scrubbing pad will take a lot of soot off, particularly if you scrub pots every meal or two. Letting the stuff build up and burn on makes the job much harder later on.

Don't forget to swish the pot scrubber very thoroughly in clean water to clear out any food particles stuck in it. The little camp thieves love to run off with a scrubber full of dinner crumbs!

Before you start down the trail again, take a long last look at the campsite. Did you leave anything behind? Are you packing out any foil or metal you brought in? If you used a fire, is it completely out?

Drowning a fire thoroughly is very important. Otherwise, coals which retain heat for many hours can be fanned by a freaky breeze into a roaring flame again long after you're gone. Fill a pot with water and use your hand to sprinkle the water evenly over the entire fire area. Water poured directly on the coals often will send a cloud of ashes straight up into your face. Sprinkling water a little at a time avoids this.

If you did use a fire, did you remember to burn your used toilet tissue in it? Burning is by far the best way to dispose of it. As you explore the woods and mountains, you'll be continually impressed by the durability of today's toilet paper—it will not stay buried and takes a long time to bio-degrade. We've decided to refold our used tissue, soiled side in, and tuck it in a small plastic bag convenient in an outer pack pocket. Then, when we can dispose of it by burning, we do.

A final look now. The fire is out, nothing is left behind, and the site's a little cleaner than you found it, just the way you'd like to find the next one.

BACKPACKING FOODS

AND RECIPES

AN INTRODUCTION TO
FOODS USED IN THIS COOKBOOK

Most of the books on backpacking listed on pages 139 and 140 contain long lists of foods adaptable to backpack munchery and cookery. All lists are less than complete, as new items are introduced each season and old ones dropped. A comprehensive list would probably contain thousands of items.

We do want to tell you about some of the less familiar foods we use in our recipes. Some of them are available in supermarkets as shown by the (S) following the item name. Others we buy only from mountaineering shops (MS) or from mail order food outlets (MO). You may also notice that some health food and natural food stores in your community stock some of these foods too.

Applesauce, evaporated. (S) Moist granules of apple, low-priced. Can be eaten as is, or added to cereals. For applesauce, add a little margarine, cinnamon, and brown sugar. Cooking time can be halved by soaking in hot water to cover for at least a half hour.

Bacon bar, Wilson's. (MS) (MO) Condensed prefried bacon, ready to eat as is or to crumble into cooked foods.

Cheddar cheese powder. (MO) Strong cheddar flavor, very useful when fresh cheese might spoil or be too heavy and bulky. Stir into one-pot meals, cream soup mixes, and egg dishes. Store airtight. Mail order places usually will sell only in No. 10 cans. Mountaineering shops sell this product in plastic bags as "instant cheese spread" (includes dry milk).

Date nuggets or pieces. (MS) (MO) Tiny chunks of dehydrated dates, a sweet, flavorful addition to cereals, syrups, puddings, cakes, and so on.

Eggs, dried, whole or whites only. (S) (MS) (MO) Several brands are commonly available in 1 lb cans. The flavor varies from brand to brand; try several. Add to drink mixes and main dishes for extra protein. Tin should be refrigerated after opening, and any meals using egg powder should be made up just before the trip, sealed well, and used on that trip.

Gum tragacanth. A flavorless thickening powder obtained from Old World leguminous herbs. We found ours at a drugstore, but had to ask for it. ¼ tsp added to dry ingredients will thicken 8 oz of liquid to milkshake consistency.

Lemon juice crystals. (S) Available in boxes of tiny foil packets, each equal to 2 tbsp lemon juice. Really perks up the flavor of too-sweet or too-bland foods. The brand in our area is Lecroy Lemon Tree.

Mushrooms, freeze-dried. (S) Schilling is the brand in our area, or you may buy in No. 10 cans from mail order places. As a substitute, Asian or European dried mushrooms may be used in backpack recipes; they are quite commonly found in supermarkets. However, they need to be soaked for several hours, then cooked along with the rice or noodles.

Meat, freeze-dried. (MS) Small packets. (MO) No. 10 cans. We regularly use the chunks of beef, chicken, corned beef, and meatballs. A 1 oz package will satisfy the desire of two to four average hikers for a few pieces of meat in each serving. Cost and limitations of flavor and texture rule out freeze-dried meat as the principal source of protein for hikers. The ham and corned beef are full-flavored, but the chicken, beef, and meatballs are much better when bouillon is added to the rehydrating water.

Meat, imitation, or Textured Vegetable Protein (TVP). (MS) (MO) Highly processed soy protein, textured and flavored to resemble beef, chicken, ham, bacon, and burger mix. The flavor and texture are improved if the chunks or granules simmer in a flavorful bouillon or sauce for at least 15 minutes. Keep in mind that soy protein is not complete protein. The missing essential amino acids can come from milk, cheese, or eggs eaten in the same meal.

Millet meal. Can be substituted for stone-ground cornmeal in most recipes. The flavor is sweeter and amino acid balance is significantly better. Look for it in natural foods stores.

Milk, dry low-fat instant. (S) Commonly available in 1 qt envelopes. Has a richer taste than non-fat milk and slightly more protein per pound. Reconstitutes more easily than whole dry milk. Store in airtight containers until used.

Milk, dry non-fat non-instant. More compact and less granular than the familiar instant non-fat milk. This form is easier to use when blended with other dry ingredients, but harder to reconstitute without lumps. Available at natural food stores.

Milk, dry whole non-instant. (MS) (MO) The 27.5% dry weight butterfat content compared to .7%-.8% for non-fat and 5% for low-fat gives this milk a very rich taste and makes it a good source of calories as well as protein. The brands we've tried do require care in reconstituting without lumps (see page 43, chain shaker). Also available in natural food stores.

Pasta, vegetable-flavored. Available in natural food stores and some supermarkets in several shapes and flavored with spinach, tomato, celery-onion-garlic, or all-spinach, all-artichoke.

Pasta, whole-wheat. Also available in natural food stores and some supermarkets. The rich, nutty flavor complements other strong-flavored ingredients.

Potatoes, dehydrated, shreds or chunks. (MS) Small packets. (MO) No. 10 cans. Quick-cooking and satisfying.

Sour cream mix. (MS) Small packets. (MO) No. 10 cans. Sometimes (S) Small packets. Some few brands require milk to prepare; check label and add dry milk to dry mix.

Tomato crystals. (MS) As "instant tomato juice" in small packets. (MO) No. 10 cans. Makes remarkably fresh-tasting tomato juice, sauce, or paste. Caution: tomato crystals absorb moisture from the air rapidly and must be stored in airtight containers.

Vegetables, freeze-dried. (MS) Small packets. (MO) No. 10 cans, and sometimes in bulk in natural food stores. Package quantities, rehydration procedures vary widely with manufacturer; check label and adapt recipe procedure to give adequate cooking time. Some suppliers offer similar-looking packets of dehydrated vegetables along with the freeze-dried ones—read labels carefully before buying. Dehydrated vegetables take much longer to rehydrate than do freeze-dried.

Whole wheat, rolled. Can be substituted in recipes calling for rolled oats. Available from natural food stores.

A PACKFUL OF COOKING TRICKS
There are some simple techniques that can save you frustration when you're handling dehydrated and freeze-dried foods.

HOW TO DEAL WITH LUMPS

Most powdered and crystallized backpacking foods get lumpy
when they're exposed to air. Leaving such foods in their
pouches or cans until cooking is the surest preventative, but
often you can't do this. Then your best defense is a double-
thickness or very heavy gauge plastic bag, or one of the tough
"boil-in" or "roast-in" bags. Press out all air and close tightly.

When you have lumps anyway, consider:

Smashing. Many lumps respond to this simple technique.
Open bag and reclose, creating some slack, airless space for
working room. Gently squeeze and rub the contents between
your fingers, a bit at a time, till lumps disappear.

Beating. Some powders and crystals, however dry and
lump-free, form lumps when mixed all at once with liquid.
Mixing the liquid very gradually into the powder seems to
work best. Make a small well in the center of the dry stuff
and slowly add water, incorporating more powder from the
edges to keep a sour cream consistency. Once it's all wet,
beat a few more strokes to remove any hidden lumps. Then
gradually add more liquid to thin to the desired consistency.

Shaking. The chain shaker (page 43) is great for dealing
with lumpy beverages or gravy mix. Put liquid, powder, and
chain into shaker, close *securely,* and shake furiously for a
minute or so.

WHAT ABOUT ALTITUDE
VS. COOKING TIME?

The boiling temperature of water drops roughly 10° for
every 5000 foot increase in altitude, and cooking time for
boiled or simmered food is said to double for every 5000
foot gain. If this is true, something that takes 25 minutes
to cook at sea level should need 50 minutes at 5000 feet,
and 1 hour 40 minutes at 10,000 feet. We haven't found
this to be true. In our experience, foods cooked at 10,000
feet were quite palatable after they had simmered about
twice as long as we would cook them at sea level.

HOW CAN YOU REDUCE
COOKING TIME?

Very often camp meals need to be prepared quickly. Either fuel or time may be scarce, weather threatening, or hikers very hungry and tired. Recipes which normally require a longer cooking time can be adapted at home to reduce cooking time. Presoaking foods in camp will reduce stove time, but not the actual time spent in meal preparation.

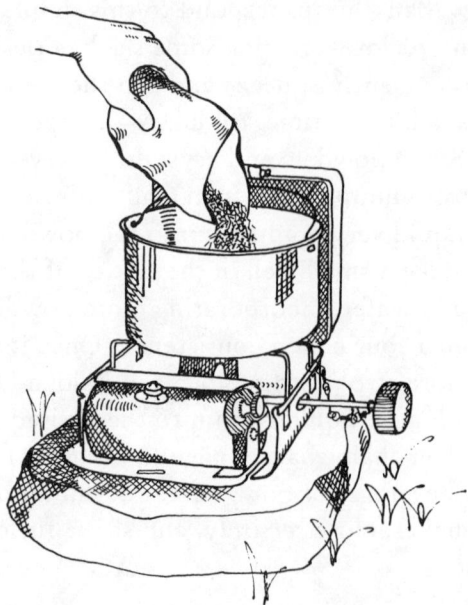

ADAPTING RECIPES

Substituting freeze-dried meat, canned meat, or Wilson's meat bars for the meat-flavored TVP called for in a recipe and also using quick brown or instant white rice in the place of long-cooking types will reduce cooking time. Instant rice needs only 5 minutes cooking time at sea level. Freeze-dried meat chunks need only about 10 minutes at sea level, compared to about 20 minutes for TVP. Substitute:

1½ cups quick brown or instant rice for 1 cup regular rice
1 or 2 oz freeze-dried meat for TVP serving 4
1 meat or bacon bar for TVP serving 2 to 4 people
(reduce salt when using bacon bar)

PRESOAKING

The cooking times for grains, dried, and freeze-dried foods can be reduced one-quarter or one-third by presoaking them in hot water for about a half hour before cooking. Meals should be bagged so that any foods to be presoaked can be separated from those requiring little or no cooking. Include the flavorings with foods to be soaked. Use boiling water in metal containers, but hot water for plastic. Reduce the amount of water you add for cooking by about the amount you used for soaking. Breakfast cereal can be soaked overnight in a bag tucked into your pack, or in a covered pot hung in a tree. Don't soak pasta—it turns gummy.

BREAKFAST

Morning air! If men will not drink of this
at the fountainhead of the day, why then
we must bottle some and sell it in the shops.
  —Henry Thoreau, *Walden*

Most breakfasts are eaten quickly as you stand shivering in
the early morning chill eager to get on the trail. Quick satis-
faction and energy is what you need. Hot cereal loaded with
raisins and nuts, or granola doused with reconstituted dry
milk makes a quick starter. As long as you're boiling water
anyway, you can easily have either coffee or tea, but don't
forget cocoa. A steaming cup of cocoa will pack more trail
calories than either tea or coffee. If you would miss your
early morning fruit juice, be sure and take along some of
the vitamin C enriched morning drinks, too.

Some days will be lay-overs. Days for slow, leisurely
breakfast. This is the time for griddle cakes, omelets, and
fresh-baked coffee cakes.

If you or someone in your group just doesn't ever eat
breakfast, forget it. Don't call it "breakfast." Have a chunk
of high-energy bread, some super cookies, a milkshake drink
—almost any lunch food that appeals—but don't start up
that trail with an empty fuel tank.

CRUNCHY GRANOLA

Making granola can be a creative experience, an opportunity to express yourself—always unique, never quite the same twice.

Find a shallow baking pan, 9 in. x 13 in. or a little larger. Preheat the oven to 325° F. Into the pan pour:

> 3 cups rolled oats*
> 1 cup grated coconut*
> ½ cup wheat germ*
> 1 cup chopped nuts* (walnuts, almonds, soy beans, etc.)
> 1 cup rolled wheat
> ½ cup sunflower seeds
> ½ cup sesame seeds

*The items marked with an asterisk are basic foundation foods of granola; the others may be omitted. Other grains, seeds, or nuts may also be included to create different tastes and textures.

In a small saucepan, heat together:

> ¼ cup margarine or oil
> ¼ tsp salt
> ¾ cup brown sugar
> 1 tsp water

Pour the sugar mixture over the grains, blending well. Toast in oven for about 40 minutes, stirring every 10 minutes. Granola will be golden and crisp, but not burned. Store, when cool, in a jar with a tight lid.

NUTTY FAMILIA

Find a gallon-size wide-mouth jar with a screw-top lid to make and store the familia in. (These jars can be had, free, at most hot dog stands.)

66

Mix together:

> 1 cup quick oatmeal
> 1 cup rolled whole wheat
> 1 cup wheat germ
> 1 cup chopped nuts
> ½ cup raisins
> ⅔ cup brown sugar

Makes about 5 cups cereal.

Both familia and granola are usually eaten with milk. You may want to add the dry milk powder to them at home to save a little hassle in camp. Then at breakfast time, just add a little water to your bowl of cereal. For 5 cups of familia add 1½ cups dry milk.

REAL OATMEAL

In this time of pasty instant hot cereals, have you forgotten the true integrity of real oatmeal?

Measure and bag:

> **2 cups regular, slow-cooking oats**
> **½ tsp salt**

To prepare:

Measure 4 cups of water into the pot and bring it to a brisk boil. If you're planning to add Breakfast Gorp, add it now and let it simmer a bit before you add the oats. Once the oats are added, stir the whole pot vigorously for a minute or two, then lower the heat and cover pot. Let it cook for a few minutes until the oats are tender. Stir it from time to time; oatmeal tends to stick to the bottom of the pot. When you decide it's done, stir in 1 or 2 tbsp of margarine. Serve with sugar and reconstituted dry milk.

Serves about 1½ Sierra cups to 4 people.

CINNAMONED RICE

Don't overlook rice as you plan hot cereal breakfasts—it makes a good change of both flavor and texture.

Measure and bag:

> 1 cup converted long grain rice
> ¼ cup raisins
> 1 tsp ground cinnamon
> ¼ tsp salt

To prepare:

Heat about 2½ cups of water to boiling. Add rice mixture and lower heat. Cook until rice is tender. Stir in about 1 tbsp of margarine. Serve with sugar and reconstituted dry milk.

Serves about 4 Sierra-cup portions.

BREAKFAST GORP

This multi-purpose food mixture adds new tastes and textures to breakfast dishes. Like other gorp mixtures, it may include different things at different times. In general, breakfast gorp is made up of one or more dried fruits and some kind of nuts. Sometimes it is bagged with sugar and sometimes without.

OUR FAVORITE

Bag together:

> 1 cup raisins
> 1 cup date nuggets
> 1 cup chopped cashews
> 1 cup brown sugar

Plan to take about 2 oz of this mix for each 4-serving batch of cereal.

APPLE JACK GORP

Bag together:

>1 cup evaporated apples
>1 tsp cinnamon
>1 cup raisins
>1 cup chopped walnuts
>1 cup white or brown sugar

WHOLE-WHEAT PANCAKES

These full-flavored pancakes make hearty breakfast fare and also can double as dessert.

Measure and bag together:

> ½ cup whole-wheat flour
> ½ cup enriched white flour
> 2 tsp baking powder
> 2 tbsp sugar
> ½ tsp salt
> ¼ cup dry milk
> ¼ cup whole dried egg

At the campsite:

Stir in about ¾ cup of water, adding it a little at a time to make a medium-thin batter. Blend in about 2 tbsp melted margarine.

To bake, first melt a little margarine in your frypan or pot lid. Spoon 2 or 3 small pools of batter into the pan when the margarine is bubbling. Small, 2 or 3 inch in diameter cakes are easy to turn and cook quickly. When cakes begin to look dry around the edges and bubbles of batter burst in the middle, they're ready to turn. Use a sawed-off rubber scraper and a spoon to turn them, neatly.

Serves 2 or 3 hikers.

MILLET PANCAKES

Millet is available at health food stores. It makes a sweet, crunchy pancake with an especially good amino acid balance.

Put together in one bag:

> ⅓ cup whole dried egg
> ½ cup non-fat dry milk
> 1 cup coarsely ground millet meal
> ⅓ cup soy flour or whole-wheat flour
> ½ tsp salt
> 1½ tsp baking powder

To prepare:

Melt 4 tbsp margarine. While it is melting, mix enough water into the mix to make a creamy batter—about 1 cup or a little more. Stir in the melted margarine. Pour by spoonfuls onto the frypan. Bake these small pancakes a little more slowly than you would cakes made with a regular flour batter. If you must let this batter stand after it's mixed, you may need to add more water.

Makes about 30-40 two-inch pancakes.

BUCKWHEAT PANCAKES

These were standard breakfast fare for old-time Westerners, and the recipe was carried all over the world by nineteenth century tourists.

Measure and bag together:

> ¾ cup buckwheat flour
> ¾ cup enriched all-purpose flour
> ½ tsp salt
> ⅓ cup dried whole egg
> ½ cup non-fat dried milk
> 1½ tsp baking powder

In camp:

Melt 4 tbsp margarine. While the margarine melts, blend about 1½ cups of water into the ingredients from the bag to make a creamy batter. Add the melted fat gradually. Bake in small cakes.

Makes about 30-40 two-inch pancakes. Excellent with berry jam or sweetened, stewed berries.

PANCAKE SYRUPS

BASIC

> 1 cup brown sugar
> ¼ cup water
> 2 tbsp margarine

Heat till bubbly and slightly thickened.

BREAKFAST GORP SYRUP

> 1½ cups Breakfast Gorp
> (raisins, dates, nuts, brown sugar)
> A spoonful of water to moisten

Heat till sugar is melted and gorp is hot.

FRUIT SYRUP

> ¼ cup evaporated apples
> 1 cup brown sugar
> ¼ tsp cinnamon
> 2 tbsp margarine
> 1 cup water

Simmer the apples first in water till they are rehydrated. Add the remaining ingredients and simmer until sugar is melted.

MUSHROOM OMELET

This more substantial omelet could be served at dinner as well as breakfast.

Measure, blend, and bag:

> 1 cup whole dried egg
> ¼ cup dry milk
> 1 tsp salt

Bag separately:

> ½ cup dehydrated sour cream
> or 2 pkg sour cream mix
> ½ cup freeze-dried mushrooms

To prepare:

Pour cold water over the mushrooms to cover and soak for 5 minutes. Blend the sour cream with cool water to make a thick paste and set aside. Mix egg mixture with 2 cups of water. Melt 1 or 2 spoonfuls of margarine in the frypan and pour in egg mixture. Cook gently, trying to keep the cooked portion together. When omelet is set, spread half the sour cream and mushrooms on one-half and fold the other hald over it. Spoon remaining sour cream and mushrooms over the top.

Serves 3 or 4.

SCRAMBLED EGGS

The whole dried eggs we've used have a good "fresh egg" flavor, and scrambled eggs have become one of our favorite trail breakfasts.

Measure, blend together very thoroughly, and bag:

> 1 cup whole dried egg
> ¼ cup dry milk
> (whole dry milk is extra good)
> 1 tsp salt

To cook:

Add 2 cups of water to egg mix a little at a time. A chain shaker or wire whisk will speed up the blending process and help you avoid lumps. Melt about 1 tbsp of margarine in the frypan. When it is bubbling, pour in the egg mixture. With a spoon pull the cooked portions together and let the liquid egg mixture flow onto the exposed pan. Continue cooking till eggs are done as you like them.

Serves 4.

EXTRA- NOURISHING BREADS

*...it was no little amusement to bake several
small loaves ... in succession, tending and
turning them as carefully as an Egyptian his
hatching eggs.*
　　　　　—Henry Thoreau, *Walden*

Breads are a compact versatile source of nourishment. Trail
breads need to be firm, solid loaves that won't crumble and
fall apart in your pack. Fruit and nut loaves generally have
that quality of moist denseness, and we've chosen only a few
to share with you.

Yeast breads made of whole grains and further enriched
with generous dollops of wheat germ and soy powder also
make good travelers. Spread with margarine and peanut
butter, they help add the needed fats and some more protein to your diet.

Then there are the breads that are baked to a rock hard-
ness and so full of dried fruits, nuts, and goodies that they
make you think of Christmas. These breads are the ones that
will last through a really long trip, doling out calories as you
need them.

All these loaves need to be well wrapped in plastic wrap
or foil, and then again in a plastic bag. Slices may be cut or
broken as you want them.

HONEY BANANA BREAD

This moist, nourishing loaf tastes so good you'll make it even when a backpacking trip isn't part of your plans.

> 2 or 3 ripe bananas
>   (enough to make 1 cup)
> 1 tsp baking soda
> ¼ cup unflavored yogurt
> ¼ cup margarine or butter
> ¼ cup honey
> ¾ cup granulated sugar
> 1 egg
> 1 cup whole-wheat flour
> ¼ cup wheat germ
> ¼ cup enriched flour
> ½ tsp salt
> ¾ cup chopped nuts, walnuts,
>   pecans, or whatever you like

Grease the inside of 3 small loaf pans (3 in. x 6 in.) or 1 regular pan (5 in. x 9 in.) with any convenient shortening and preheat oven to 350° F. Beat bananas to a pulpy foam, add baking soda, stir well, and set aside. Cream together in a large mixing bowl yogurt, margarine, honey, and sugar. Beat in egg. Add alternately with the banana mixture the remaining ingredients. Divide dough evenly into the 3 pans, or spread in the one large one. Bake for about an hour or until loaves test done. Let loaves cool for a few minutes in their pans, then turn out onto a cake rack. Loaves can be returned to their pans for freezing or storing.

Makes 3 trail lunch loaves of about 3 servings each.

LOGAN BREAD

A favorite of the U.C. Berkeley Hiking Club for many years.

Into a large mixing bowl, dump:

> 1 cup enriched flour, OR ½ cup flour,
>   ½ cup soy flour, and ¼ cup wheat germ
> 4 cups whole-wheat flour or graham flour
> 1 cup honey
> 3 tbsp molasses
> ¾ cup brown sugar
> ½ to ¾ cup dry milk
> ¼ cup salad oil
> 1 tsp salt
> 1 tsp baking powder
> 2 to 4 cups dried fruit and nuts (raisins, apricots,
>   walnuts, sesame seeds, and so forth)

Mix all these ingredients together, using your hands. The dough will be very stiff, but only add water if it won't stick together at all without it. Pat or roll out on cookie sheets to a thickness of about ½ inch. Score into squares with a sharp knife before baking. Bake 1 hour at 300° F.

Makes 2 about 9 in. x 13 in. pans.

BREAD EVERLASTING

This one's from Ruth Cross, a Generation I member of the Cross family. It is reminiscent of holiday cakes, yet still "bread" enough to be good spread with margarine. Best of all, as long as there's any left, it'll be moist and tender.

Cream together well:

> 1 cup brown sugar
> 1 cup granulated sugar
> 1 cup vegetable shortening

In another large bowl blend:

> 1 generous cup of raisins
> 1 cup chopped nuts
> 1 cup glaceed fruits
> 1 cup cut-up dates

These fruit and nut quantities may be cut in half and the bread will still still be good. Mix well into fruit mixture:

> 1 tsp salt
> 1 tsp cinnamon
> ½ tsp ground cloves
> ½ tsp ground allspice
> ½ cup whole dry milk
> 3 tsp soda
> 4¼ cups whole-wheat flour

In another small bowl mix:

> 2 cups water
> 2 tbsp vinegar

Add the dry ingredients and this liquid alternately to the sugar/fat mixture until all is well blended. Divide into two well-greased 9 in. x 5 inc. loaf pans and bake about 1 hour at 325° F. or until done. The time will vary depending on the fruits used. Cool on a cake rack and cut each loaf into 3 or 5 chunks for trail lunches.

WHOLE-WHEAT TRAIL BREAD

Assemble an electric mixer and use the larger bowl. Measure into it:

> 2¼ cups tap water, about 115° F.
> 1 heaping tbsp dry active yeast

Set beaters on slow speed and continue beating as you add:

> 2 tsp salt
> ½ cup dry milk
> 2 tbsp honey
> 2 tbsp molasses
> ¼ cup white sugar
> ½ cup vegetable shortening
> 2 whole eggs

When all these ingredients are mixed together well, add:

> 3 cups enriched white all-purpose flour

Beat at a medium speed for about 5 minutes. Measure into another large bowl:

> 2 cups whole-wheat flour
> ½ cup wheat germ

Pour the yeast mixture over the flour in the second bowl and blend very thoroughly till you can't see any more flour. Cover and let rise in a warm place for about an hour. Turn dough out onto a well-floured surface and knead with vigor. Divide the well-kneaded dough into 6 equal portions and shape as you always do for loaves. Grease 6 small loaf pans (3 in. x 5 in.). Brush the tops of the loaves with oil and let rise about an hour. Bake at 375° F. for about 30 minutes or until done. Turn the loaves out onto a rack to cool. When they are cool, put them back into their pans for storage, carrying, or freezing.

STURDY GRAHAM ROUNDS

A far tastier vehicle for cheese spreads, peanut butter, jam, or hunks of salami than the traditional pilot biscuits.

4 cups graham or whole-wheat flour, unsifted
2 tbsp sugar
¼ cup water, warm
1 cake yeast or 1 tbsp dry yeast
3 tbsp melted margarine or oil
About 2½ cups unbleached, enriched
   all-purpose flour
2 cups warm water
2 tsp salt
2 tbsp instant minced onion, OR
   grated peel of 1 orange and ½ tsp cumin

Dissolve yeast and sugar in ¼ cup water; let proof while measuring graham flour, ½ cup all-purpose flour, salt, onion, or spice into large mixing bowl. Add yeast to bowl along with margarine and 2 cups water. Beat very thoroughly with wire whip, electric mixer, or something like that for 3 minutes. Add 1½ cups more all-purpose flour, mixing with heavy spoon. Turn out dough onto floured board, knead until smooth and elastic (about 10 minutes), adding more flour as needed. Put dough in oiled bowl, cover, let rise until doubled.

Punch dough down, divide into 24 equal parts. Shape each part into a ball. Starting with the first shaped ball, flatten each to ½-inch thickness. Let rise on greased cookie sheets until doubled, about 30 minutes. Bake at 425° F. until lightly browned. Remove from oven and cool on baking rack. When cool enough to handle, split like English muffins, using 2 forks. Return halves cut side up to oven set at 150-200° F. and dry until crisp throughout, about 2-3 hours.

Makes 48 rounds.

SUPER COOKIES

These little goodies are a lift to the spirits as well as to the body and carry well in rough conditions. Some of the recipes are for old favorites, but with an important difference. Along with the familiar flavorings, we've slipped in an extra serving of important nutrients. You may want to wrap the cookies by twos and threes for easy dividing among lunch bags. Or if you plan on a batch of cookies for a dinner dessert, wrap a bunch of them together.

PEANUT BUTTER COOKIES WITH CRUNCH

Never thought I'd find a peanut butter cookie to make me give up the ones Mother used to make, but I did, and here it is.

> 1 cup margarine
> 1 cup chunky, salted peanut butter
> ¾ cup granulated sugar
> 1 cup brown sugar, packed
> 2 eggs
> 1 tsp vanilla
> 2 cups whole-wheat flour
> 2 tsp baking powder
> 2 cups granola

Cream margarine, peanut butter, sugars thoroughly together. Add eggs and vanilla and beat well. Mix in flour and baking powder, then add granola. 1 cup of raisins can be added if you like. Drop dough from teaspoon onto greased cookie sheets. Flatten each cookie in crisscross pattern with a fork dipped in flour. Bake at 350° F. until lightly browned, about 10 minutes.

HONEY-NUT COOKIE BARS

A dense, chewy trail cookie that offers lots of food value and a not-so-sweet, nutty flavor.

Preheat oven to 350° F. and oil a 9 in. x 13 in. baking pan. Separate 2 eggs, setting the whites aside. Beat together:

> 2 egg yolks
> ⅔ cup honey

Combine well:

> 4 tbsp non-fat dry milk
> ¼ cup whole-wheat flour
> ¼ cup tsp salt
> ½ tsp coriander
> ¼ tsp nutmeg
> 1 tsp baking powder

Add dry ingredients to honey mixture and blend well. Then add:

> 1 cup chopped walnuts or almonds
> ¾ cup unhulled sesame seeds

Mix well. Beat egg whites until they hold stiff peaks and fold into dough. Spread batter in pan and bake 25-30 minutes. Cool in pan, then cut into bars.

OATMEAL-PLUS COOKIES

A chewy cookie that will remind you of when you were a kid, but this one's super-charged with calories and good nutrition.

Blend together by hand or with an electric mixer at slow blending speed:

> ¼ lb margarine
> 1 cup brown sugar, firmly packed

Add each of the ingredients listed below as the preceding one disappears:

> 1 egg
> 1 tsp vanilla
> 1 cup whole-wheat flour
> ½ tsp soda
> ½ tsp salt
> ½ tsp baking powder
> 1 cup rolled oats
> ½ cup chopped nuts
> ½ cup grated coconut
> ¾ cup raisins

Drop by generous teaspoons onto greased cookie sheets. Bake about 12 minutes in a 350° F. oven.

Makes 3 dozen.

BROWNIES

Preheat the oven to 350° F. and grease a 9 in. x 9 in. pan.

½ cup butter
½ cup granulated sugar
½ cup honey
2 eggs
2 squares unsweetened chocolate, melted
½ tsp vanilla
⅔ cup whole-wheat flour
¼ cup wheat germ
2 tbsp soy flour
¼ cup non-fat dry milk
Pinch salt
½ cup chopped nuts

Cream together butter, sugar, and honey. Add eggs, chocolate, and vanilla, beating well. Stir in the remaining ingredients and beat until well blended. Bake at 350° F. about 35 minutes, or until done. When the brownies are cool, cut into squares and wrap in plastic wrap. Then bag and tie.

A WHITE GAS STOVE
(optimus)

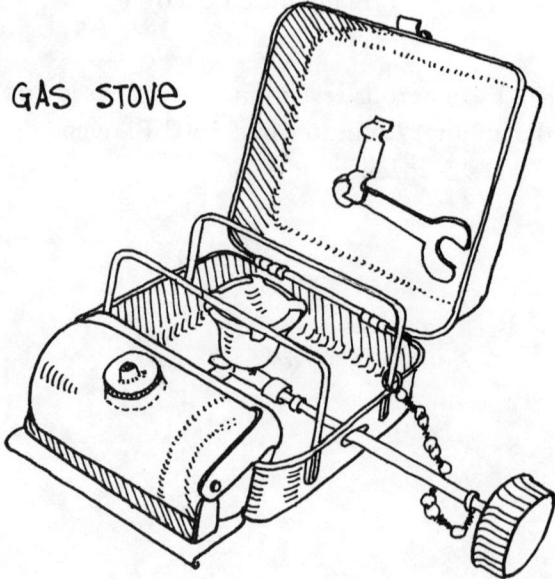

86

LUNCH

GORP

Like most recipes from Ye Goode Olde Hikynge Daies, the
formula for gorp has been modified a thousand times. Broadly
defined, gorp is a mix of small pieces of dry, ready-to-munch
foods chosen for high energy value and a good taste blend.
Most of the traditional recipes include M&M's, peanuts and
raisins in varying proportions. Some later recipes include
over ten ingredients. Whatever mixture you create, include
something sweet for quick energy, something rich for staying
power, and something salty to help rehydration. Here are
some variations we've encountered:

Nutty-Fruity Gorp. 1 cup *each* toasted sunflower seeds,
  dried pineapple, mixed freeze-dried fruit bits or freeze-
  dried fruit cocktail, salted peanuts, raisins.
Good Old Gorp. 1 cup *each* salted peanuts, caramel corn
  (only for those few who can abide it), M&M's, roasted
  cashews, 2 cups raisins.
Sweet-Tooth Gorp. 1 cup *each* M&M's, spice gumdrops,
  roasted peanuts.
Elegant Gorp. 1 cup *each* raisins, roasted cashews, Cheesits
  (or tiny Japanese rice crackers), cream caramels.

Got the idea? The possible combinations are endless. Just
leave wrapped anything whose flavor or texture might suffer
from too much togetherness (like small hard candies or gourmet cheese cubes), and don't include anything overpowering
like salami unless you and your friends don't mind having
everything in the gorp taste of it.

HIGH-ENERGY BARS

POW BARS

½ cup honey or molasses
½ cup real peanut butter, crunchy or smooth
1 cup or a little more dry milk—non-instant
    is easiest to work with

Knead these ingredients together with your hands, adding enough milk powder to form a stiff but not crumbly dough. Chocolate bits, raisins or other dried fruit, coconut can be kneaded in as well. Or you can use cashew or almond butter in place of the peanut butter. Shape into logs about 2-3 in. long and about 1 in. in diameter and roll in powdered milk, confectioner's sugar, or coconut.

    Makes about 6.

CHOCOLATE CRUNCH BARS

½ cup honey
⅓ cup margarine
¼ cup sweetened cocoa powder or
    carob powder
1 cup crunchy granola
1 cup or more dry milk

Blend together the honey, margarine, cocoa, and milk to form a stiff dough. Knead in the granola, or roll shaped bars in granola.

APRICOT BOMBS

These are delicious, but sticky. Package them separately, and put a little extra powdered sugar in the bag.

> 8 oz moist dried apricots
> ¼ cup coconut
> 2 tbsp orange marmalade
> 4 tsp powdered milk
> Optional: 4 tsp roasted sunflower seeds,
>   sesame seeds, or chopped nuts

Steam apricots if they are stiff to soften them. Put apricots through grinder, using finest blade, or chop very fine. Mix and mash apricots together with remaining ingredients, using wooden spoon with vigor. Shape into 1-inch balls, roll in powdered sugar, coating thickly. Roll again in powdered sugar or coconut in half an hour or so.

Makes about 14.

A FEW LIGHT WEIGHT
LIDDED CONTAINERS

DATE BOMBS

Pound and mash with wooden spoon:

> 1 cup cut-up dates, firmly packed
> ½ cup walnut, sesame, or almond meal
> ½ cup coconut flakes
> (2 tsp rum or brandy)

When mixture is well blended, shape into 1-inch balls and roll in nut meal or in more coconut.

JERKY

> 1½ lb flank steak
> ¾ cup red wine
> ⅓ cup Worcestershire sauce
> 1 tsp salt
> A few grinds black pepper
> ¼ tsp garlic powder
> ½ of a large onion, sliced

Trim all the fat off the steak. Slice the meat with the grain. The grain will look like red strings. Slice it as thin as you can. Lay these strips in a casserole and marinate at room temperature overnight. Prepare the marinade by blending together the rest of the ingredients and pouring them over the meat. Cover the casserole tightly and put it out of reach of curious dogs and cats.

In the morning arrange the meat strips on cake-cooling racks or directly on the racks of the oven. Put foil or cookie sheets below the meat to catch the drips. Set the oven at 200° F. and dry the meat 8 to 10 hours. It will be very dark brown when it's done and much smaller in size. Test often toward the end of the drying time and take the jerky from the oven when it's just the way you like it best. When it's cool, bag it.

CHEDDAR CHEESE SPREAD

A hearty spread for lunchtime bread or crackers can be quickly whipped together on the trail from this mix you prepare at home. The dry mix will keep through the longest trip, and also weighs less than fresh cheese.

In a bag, mix together:

> 1 cup cheddar cheese powder
> ½ cup any powdered milk (instant skim
> makes a lumpy spread)

Add, if you wish, any combination of these:

> ½ tsp onion powder
> ½ tsp caraway seeds
> ⅛ tsp garlic powder
> 1 tbsp or more bacon-flavored bits
> ½ to 1 tsp sweet, fragrant paprika
> ½ tsp marjoram

In camp, gradually add enough water to all or part of the mix to make as much smooth paste as you wish. For all of the mix, use ½ to ¾ cup water. This amount makes about 1¼ cups spread. Then add dollops of soft margarine or butter to enrich and smooth the cheese mix. Smear on crackers or breads. Or you can stir the cheese cream into cooked potatoes, noodles, pasta, or grains.

OFF-THE-SHELF LUNCH FOOD

Lunch bags usually include quite a bit of food bought ready to eat from your grocer's shelves. Just remember to choose foods that need no more preparation than upwrapping, or mixing with water, that are compact, sturdy, and provide ample calories for their weight and bulk.

Drink mixes. Choose those "punch" mixes which contain sugar and vitamin C. Milkshake or malt mixes are a good source of calories. Both taste best when mixed with cold water; milkshake mix may be quite unpalatable when mixed with warm water. Hot soup is very welcome in cold weather; bouillons or the new instant soup mixes are the easiest to fix.

Cheese. Hunks of Parmesan, dry Monterey Jack, or well-aged cheddar will keep for at least a week in the temperatures typical of the high Sierra in summer. In warmer or more humid areas, eat fresh cheese within a few days. If you can find them, canned or individually wrapped gourmet cheese cubes will keep till the end of the week.

Meat, fish, poultry. Jerky and salami or other dry sausages are common lunch staples. Some people happily munch dried shrimp and tiny dried fish from Japanese markets. For the less adventurous, there is a vast array of potted meats, fish, and poultry products available in delicatessens or supermarkets. Only those containing very little water are worth carrying when weight and bulk matter—liverwurst spread, pâté, sardines, for example. You must be willing to carry the cans out again, though. Scrub well or burn first to remove odor.

Crackers and breads. Anything you choose should be small and hard, to resist crumbling. Tiny Japanese rice crackers, intriguingly shaped and flavored, are a nice change. Most crackers should be repackaged to reduce bulk.

Cookies and cakes. Again, the smaller and sturdier, the better they travel. Check natural food stores for sweets offering a bonus of proteins, vitamins, and minerals. In warm or humid weather, eat items with high proportions of fat and eggs early in the trip.

Candy. Fruit and sugar candies offer quick energy. Those with high proportions of nuts, seeds, or chocolate offer more nutrients and take longer to digest. Sticky candies are best when individually wrapped. Milk chocolate will melt in warm weather; semi-sweet resists heat better. Tropical chocolate, available from mountaineering shops, has a still higher melting point.

Dried fruits. In addition to the usual kinds, some natural food and gourmet stores offer dried pineapple, mango, and banana chips. All dried fruits are laxative, causing some people real distress. Try to offer an alternative food for them.

Nuts and seeds. Welcome changes from the usual kinds: roasted and salted soybeans, sunflower seeds, squash seeds, candy-coated nuts. Peanut and other nut butters can go hiking, too, in plastic tubes (see page 28). Spread them on your bread and crackers, or make Peanut Butter Soup (page 100).

Mountaineering shops and others who supply freeze-dried foods offer specialty items, like dried "ice cream," freeze-dried tuna or egg salad. Check food lists from suppliers named on page 141. Detailed lists of off-the-shelf foods are available in books on backpacking listed on pages 139 and 140. If you spend a little time wandering through your supermarket, natural food store, or delicatessen, you'll undoubtedly find other good lunch selections.

DINNERS

This is a delicious evening, when the whole body is one sense, and imbibes delight through every pore. I go and come with a strange liberty in Nature, a part of herself.
—Henry Thoreau, *Walden*

Slow down, take it easy, feast first on the view as the water pot heats. The first hot water is for drinks and/or soup to sip slowly while the second pot of water simmers dinner.

A slosh of booze in that first drink, whether it's hot or cold, may help take the edge off your tired muscles, but remember the liquor you mix into the lemonade at 9000 feet altitude will have about twice the effect it does at sea level. Take it easy, till you know how the spirits and mountain air blend within you.

If someone has hooked a fish, cook it and savor its delicate flavor first before you dig into the main dish of the evening. These entrees are planned to be both filling and strength-giving, but on some nights you may not be quite satisfied. Fruit is the common trail dessert and we've included some ways to make it especially good. Puddings also make easy trail desserts. We've found, too, that fresh-baked cakes are well worth the little extra time they take.

Then, to top it all off, we suggest a final cup of cocoa, maybe laced with a little rum, as you gaze at the stars.

AN APPETIZER AND SEVERAL SOUPS

GARLIC CRUNCH

This is a very nutritious stuff to nibble with drinks.

Combine in a shallow pan:

> ½ cup sunflower seeds
> ½ cup pumpkin seeds
> ½ cup roasted soybeans
> ½ cup chopped Virginia peanuts

Pour over this:

> 1 tbsp corn germ oil or salad oil,
> blended with ½ tsp garlic salt

Toast, shaking occasionally, in a 350° F. oven for about 20 minutes. Drain on paper towel. When cool, store in a screw-top jar. Bag for trip and serve with cold drinks.

GARDEN VEGETABLE SOUP WITH BEEF

After a few days out, most hikers begin to long for something fresh. A big cupful of these fresh-tasting freeze-dried vegetables should be a big morale-booster.

Package together:

> 2 oz freeze-dried beef, meatballs, or
>> 4 oz beef-flavored TVP
>
> 4 oz tiny bow- or shell-shaped enriched pasta
> 1 oz each freeze-dried peas, carrots, corn
> ⅜ oz freeze-dried green beans
> 1 tbsp instant minced onion
> 2 tbsp dried parsley
> ¼ cup tomato crystals
> 4 beef bouillon cubes or ¼ cup bouillon granules
> 1 tsp basil
> ⅛ tsp garlic powder
> 2 envelopes vegetable-beef soup, making 20-24 oz
>> soup each
>
> 3 oz grated Parmesan cheese in a separate bag

To prepare:

Put all ingredients but cheese in pot. Add 7 cups cold water and heat, covered, to boiling. Reduce heat and simmer 10-20 minutes or until carrots, beans, and meat are as tender as you like. Add up to 1 cup more water if soup is too thick. Serve with cheese on top.

Makes 8-9 cups.

GREEK WEDDING SOUP

Very refreshing. The flavor is rich, yet tart.

> 1 envelope chicken noodle soup mix,
>   making 4 cups soup
> 1 tbsp parsley flakes
> ⅓ cup dried whole egg powder
> 1 envelope lemon juice crystals

Package egg and parsley together and put into a bag containing the envelopes of soup and lemon. To prepare:

Follow package directions for cooking the chicken soup. Mix the dried egg with 1/3 cup of water to make a cream. When soup is cooked, slowly ladle a thin stream of soup into the egg mix, stirring the egg vigorously. Add about a cup of soup this way. Return egg-soup mix to the rest of soup, mix well. Do not cook further. Add lemon crystals and serve.

Makes 4 cups.

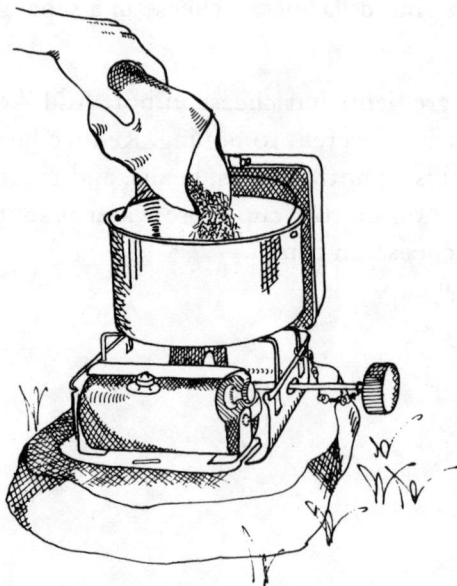

SPICY TOMATO SOUP

Weigh or measure and bag together:

> 2 oz tomato crystals
> 2 oz chicken bouillon granules or 5 cubes
>   chicken bouillon
> ½ tsp sugar
> ¼ tsp basil
> 1 tsp instant minced onion or freeze-dried chives
> 1 pkg lemon crystals
> 1 tbsp dried parsley

In camp:
    Dump into pot and gradually add 3-4 cups cold water.
Bring to boil and simmer a few minutes to blend flavors.
    Makes 3-4 cups.

HEARTY POTATO SOUP

Bag together:

> 2 slices fresh bacon, well-wrapped, or use
>   1 tbsp of a Wilson's bacon bar carried in
>   general supply
> 1 oz dehydrated onion, or 1 tsp freeze-dried
>   chives
> 5 oz dehydrated potato shreds
> 2 oz chicken bouillon granules or 5 chicken
>   bouillon cubes

Cook the bacon in the pot until it's crisp, remove and drain.
Add the onion, potato, and bouillon to the fat and slowly
add about 3 cups water—warm or hot if possible. Bring to
simmer and simmer until vegetables are tender (5-10 minutes).
Taste and add salt if needed. Serve with bacon crumbles on
top.
    Makes about 4 cups.

PEANUT BUTTER SOUP

Don't laugh; it's really quite good. The flavor is rich, creamy, mild.

Package together:

> 1 envelope cream of onion soup mix
> (making 2½ cups soup)
> ½ cup dry milk in a separate bag with
> ⅛ tsp nutmeg
> Reserve about 3 tbsp peanut butter in
> your plastic tube supply for soup

Put soup mix in pan, add 2½ cups cold water, and heat to boiling, stirring frequently. Meanwhile, mix milk powder with 1 cup water. Turn heat to low, add milk to soup. Simmer 5-10 minutes. While soup simmers, blend in peanut butter.

Makes about 4 cups.

CURRIED PEANUT BUTTER SOUP

A good lunchtime soup.

Package together:

> 1 envelope cream of onion soup mix
> (making 2½ cups soup)
> ½ cup dry milk with 1 tsp curry powder
> in a small bag
> 1 cup or more dried or freeze-dried fruit
> and nuts in a separate bag
> Reserve about 3 tbsp peanut butter for soup

Prepare as for peanut butter soup above. Serve fruits as an accompanying nibble.

SAVORY DUMPLINGS

The addition of plump, tender dumplings to a stew or soup will go a long way toward satisfying ravenous appetites.

Bag together:

> 2 cups Master Mix (p 129)
> 1 tbsp instant minced onion, toasted or plain
> 2 tbsp dried parsley
> ½ tsp sage

In camp:

Add ½ to ¾ cup water to make a stiff dough. Dip out dough by teaspoon and drop into soup or stew. Liquid should be simmering gently—too much agitation and the dumplings may break apart. Cover the pan and simmer gently until dumplings have risen and are done in the center (about 5-10 minutes).

If there isn't room in the pot for all of the dumplings in one layer, don't add a second tier. Serve the first batch with some of the soup or stew and cook a second or third batch in the remainder.

Dumplings are good with almost any soup or stew, and can be flavored in as many ways as biscuit dough. The proportions given above make enough dumplings for main dish servings for 4-5 people.

CHEESE DUMPLINGS

A richer dumpling, thanks to the cheese. The hearty cheddar flavor holds its own against pea or oxtail soup. Try these in vegetable soup, especially the Parmesan cheese version.

Measure and bag together:

> 1 cup Master Mix (page 129)
> ¼ cup powdered cheddar cheese
>   or ¼ cup grated Parmesan cheese
> ¼ tsp oregano

You can omit the cheese if you like and simply reserve at least 2 oz cheese from your fresh cheese rations for these dumplings. If fresh cheese is used, add 2 oz or more cheese crumbles or shavings to the dry mix in camp, before mixing with water.

Prepare and cook dumplings as directed in master recipe on page 101.

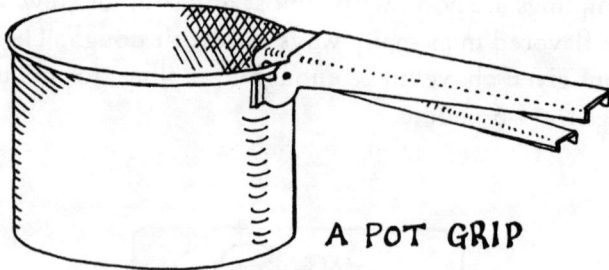

A POT GRIP

TOMATO BISQUE WITH CHEESE DUMPLINGS

In one bag measure:

> 2 oz tomato crystals
> 2 oz chicken bouillon granules or 5 cubes
>   chicken bouillon
> ½ tsp sugar
> ½ tsp basil
> 1 tsp freeze-dried chives
> 1 tbsp dried parsley

Package in a separate bag:

> **1 cup dry skim milk or ¾ cup dry whole milk**

Put these bags into a larger bag containing a bag of cheese dumpling mix (page 101). Use half of the dumpling mix recipe for a predinner soup; use the full amount for a "dumplings-with-sauce" light main dish.

In camp:
   Put contents of tomato bag in pot, add 5 cups cold water, bring to boil. When boiling, reduce heat to simmer. Meanwhile, reconstitute milk with 1 cup water to make a smooth cream. Mix dumpling batter. Add milk to simmering soup, return to simmer, add dumplings, cover, and cook 5-10 minutes.
   Makes 6-7 cups soup, not including dumplings.

PREPARING FRESH-CAUGHT PAN FISH

HEAD'S-ON STYLE
Rap the live fish firmly against a rock to stun or kill it.
Locate the anal fins. Insert the point of your knife in the
small opening located between these fins. Work carefully,
slitting only the skin, not the intestines. Continue slitting
along the underbelly toward the jaw. When you have com-
pleted this slit, the intestines will simply drop out, in a mass.
Wash the entire fish and particularly this cavity with several
changes of cold water to get all the extra stuff out.

HEAD'S-OFF METHOD
Grasping the live fish firmly in your left hand and holding
it against a tree or rock, quickly cut through the spinal cord
at the top of the head. This results in instant death and ren-
ders the fish quite motionless. Continue this cut around the
bony structure back of the gills. As you complete this cut,
almost, stop just under the lower jaw and gently pull the
entire head down. Often the guts will simply come out as
you finish severing the head. If they don't, you can always
slit as with the head's-on method.

SCALING

Some very good pan fish do have scales, which must be
scraped off before the fish is cooked. When fish are maturing
and growing, they grow scales and these little circular pieces
are simply a part of the fish's skin. They're attached on the
edge toward the fish's head and loose on the edge toward the
tail. For this reason, it's easiest to scrape them off starting
at the tail and working toward the head. It's a messy job,
but if you catch many fish that have scales, you'll become
quite adept at scaling.

STORING FISH

Sometimes the fishermen in your party will get lucky *after*
dinner and return to camp at bedtime with a nice string of
fish. The safest thing to do when this happens is to clean the
fish very carefully and thoroughly, submerge them in a pot
of the coldest water you can find, and hang that pot from a
high limb of a tree.

   We have another solution for this problem in our family.
We simply clean the fish, cook them, and enjoy a second,
bedtime dinner. This is probably the safest method of fish
storage you're likely to find.

THE BASIC FISH FRY

All fishermen have their favorite, simple routines for preparing freshly caught fish—and all are likely to be succulent.

ONE METHOD

Melt a spoonful of margarine in the frypan or pot lid. When
it is bubbly, add the cleaned fish. Adjust the heat to a low
simmer. Brown fish on one side and then turn it over gently.
Cover the pan for a minute or two. Don't overcook fish. It's
done when the meat falls in flakes as you press it lightly
with a spoon. Serve with more melted margarine, salt, pepper,
and lemon crystals.

ANOTHER METHOD

Dip the cleaned fish in a bit of flour or cornmeal and fry as
above.

FISH POACHING

Melt a spoonful of margarine in the pan and add 1 or 2
packets of lemon crystals and about half a cup of water.
Arrange fish in the liquid and sprinkle with salt and pepper.
Lower heat and cover the pan. Simmer very gently for 4
or 5 minutes, or until done. If you've carried some white
wine, substitute a bit of it for the lemon juice and poach
in the same way.

TROUT CHOWDER

After a particularly good run of fishing, chowder makes a
welcome change from the usual panfrying.

Put together in a small bag:

> 1 tbsp dried onion
> 1 tsp salt
> ⅛ tsp pepper
> 1 tsp dill weed
> ¼ tsp tarragon
> 1 tsp freeze-dried chives

Put this in a larger bag with:

> 1½ cups instant mashed potato
> 1 cup whole dry milk or
>   1 envelope Milkman
> 1 envelope lemon juice crystals

In camp:

Heat 1 quart of water and the seasoning mix to boiling.
Clean trout and cut into spoon-size pieces. When water boils,
stir in 3 tbsp margarine and the potatoes and milk, which
you have previously mixed to a cream with a little cold
water. Add trout and simmer gently until fish is done, about
5 minutes. Taste for salt, adding more to taste. Season to
taste with lemon crystals.

Makes about 5 cups, exclusive of trout.

WESTERN FISH STEW

Measure and bag together:

> 3 oz dehydrated onion
> 1 oz or 2 cubes chicken bouillon
> 1 oz or 2 cubes beef bouillon
> ¼ tsp garlic powder
> ½ tsp thyme
> 2 pkg lemon crystals
> 1 in. stick of cinnamon

Bag separately:

> 2 oz tomato crystals

Catch several fish, clean them, remove all bones, and cut into chunks.

To prepare:
  Add the contents of the first bag to 4 or 5 cups of water and simmer gently for 10 to 15 minutes. Blend the tomato crystals with enough cool water to form a smooth paste. Add this paste slowly to the simmering broth. Blend broth well and taste. Adjust seasoning as needed. Then add fish and cook only until it flakes easily.
  Serves 3 or 4.

"THE-ONE-THAT-GOT-AWAY" CHOWDER

  "It was that long, honest . . . " Sometimes the best of fishermen return to camp with empty stringers. For just such times, carry along a couple of cans of minced clams, whole shrimp, or oysters.
  Prepare the Trout Chowder (page 106) but add the canned fish when the potatoes are ready and heat only long enough to warm the fish.

ONE-KETTLE ENTREES

CHEESE AND RICE

This is a fast, basic dish we never get tired of.

Weigh and bag:

> 4½ oz dehydrated cheddar cheese

Bag separately:

> 3¾ oz instant rice

To prepare:

Bring about 3 cups of water to a boil and add the rice and a sprinkle of salt. Simmer gently till rice is tender. Stir in cheese and add a big spoonful of margarine from the general supply. Cover the pot and let stand a minute or two to rehydrate the cheese and melt the margarine.

Makes about 4 Sierra cups.

CHEESE AND RICE PLUS

A variation on the theme; you will probably think of others.

Bag the cheese as you did for Cheese and Rice. Weigh and bag:

> 3¾ oz instant rice
> ½ oz dehydrated onions

Also bag:

> 1¾ oz soy ham, or take 1 pkg freeze-dried ham
> 1 oz freeze-dried green beans (if you bought in
>   bulk) or 1 pkg

In camp:

Heat about 4 cups of water and dip out enough to rehydrate the freeze-dried foods. To the remaining water in the pot add rice and onions (also soy ham, if you are using it). Simmer until tender. Add freeze-dried ham, beans, a spoonful of margarine, and cheese. Stir well. Cover and simmer at a very low heat for a minute or two.

Makes 4 or 5 Sierra cups.

MACARONI AND BEEF SIMPLE SUPPER

The hearty flavors appeal to hungry hikers, and the simple preparation appeals to the cook.

Bag together:

> 9 oz whole-wheat or enriched elbow macaroni
> 2 oz freeze-dried beef chunks or
>   4 oz beef-flavored TVP
> 4 cubes beef bouillon or ¼ cup bouillon granules
> 2 oz tomato crystals
> 1 tsp each basil, oregano
> ¼ tsp garlic powder

Put this in a bag together with:

> 1 envelope cream of onion soup mix
>   (making 2½ cups)
> 1 pkg freeze-dried corn

To prepare:

Bring 7 cups water to boil. Add macaroni-meat mixture and simmer 10 minutes. While macaroni cooks, mix about ½ cup cold water into soup. Add soup to pot, cook dish 5-10 minutes longer, or until macaroni and meat are tender. Corn should be added either at the end or cooked with meat and macaroni, depending on the directions given for rehydration.

Makes 8-8½ cups.

HAM AND POTATOES AU GRATIN

Sometimes we overlook potatoes. They are a food that has taken to dehydration with little loss of flavor—and they're good for a change.

Weigh and bag together:

> 8 oz dehydrated potato shreds
> 2 oz soy ham nuggets*
> 1 oz dried green pepper
> 1 oz dehydrated onions
> 1 oz freeze-dried green beans

*You may want to substitute freeze-dried ham dices. If so, follow the procedure for rehydrating them in their own packet.

Bag separately:

> 8 oz dehydrated cheddar cheese

In camp:

Measure about 4 cups of water into the pot and bring to a boil. Add all the ingredients in the first bag and simmer gently, adding a little water if needed, about 20 minutes or until the potatoes are tender. Add a spoonful of margarine and check the seasoning. It will probably need some salt. Add cheese and blend well. Add ham now if you're using freeze-dried dices. Cover and heat for a minute.

Serves 4, or about 8 Sierra cups.

CHICKEN CREAM WITH VEGETABLES AND DUMPLINGS

Make the dumplings small; they'll puff up huge and light at high altitudes.

Bag together:

> 1 pkg leek soup mix, making 4½ cups soup
> 2 oz freeze-dried chicken or
>   4 oz chicken-flavored TVP
> 1 oz each freeze-dried carrots, green beans, peas
> 4 cubes chicken bouillon or ¼ cup bouillon
>   granules
> 1 tsp dill weed
> ½ tsp tarragon
> 1 recipe Savory Dumplings (page 101) in a
>   separate bag
> ¾ cup dry milk powder in a separate bag

To prepare:

Add 5 cups cold water to all but dumplings and milk. Bring to boil, stirring regularly. Simmer 10 minutes. Prepare dumpling dough as directed. Mix ½ cup water with milk powder; add to soup gradually, then spoon in dumplings and cook as directed, with pot covered and liquid just simmering. Margarine can be stirred into soup to enrich it just before adding dumplings.

Makes at least 8 cups.

CHICKEN CURRY

This one can be ready to serve in 15 minutes. The first time we cooked it was on the trail one night when we had to recharge our energy in a hurry and make it on to a campsite before dark.

Bag together:

> 6 oz instant rice
> 1 oz or 2 cubes chicken bouillon
> 1 tsp curry (in a twist of plastic wrap)
> 1 pkg freeze-dried chicken
> 1 pkg cream of mushroom soup mix

Bag together, or separately, the condiments:

> 3 oz grated coconut
> 7 oz salted peanuts
> 1 cup or a little more raisins

Put all these in one dinner bag.

To prepare:

Bring 5 or 6 cups of water and the soup mix to a simmer. Add rice and bouillon. Simmer gently for a few minutes. When rice is almost tender, add chicken. Continue simmering a minute or two more until all seems done. Add curry powder to taste and check to see if more salt is needed. Serve along with coconut, peanuts, and raisins.

Makes about 8 Sierra cups, or 4 servings.

SPINACHBURGER SPECIAL

A rich-tasting dish, especially filling when made with meat bars.

Package together:

> 1 cup beef-flavored **TVP** or 1 or 2 Wilson's
>   meat bars, left in their foil envelopes
> 3 tbsp instant minced onion
> 1 tsp basil
> ¼ to ½ tsp garlic powder
> 4 beef bouillon cubes or ¼ cup bouillon granules
> 2 cups quick brown rice
> ½ cup tomato crystals
> 1½ oz spinach flakes in separate bag
> 2 oz grated **Parmesan** cheese in separate bag

In camp:

Crumble meat bar(s), if used, into pot and brown lightly over medium heat. Add 6 cups water and remaining ingredients except spinach and cheese. If using soy beef, simply add cold water to all ingredients but spinach and cheese. Bring to boil, lower heat and simmer 20-30 minutes, or until rice and soy beef are tender. Add spinach flakes about 10 minutes before dish is done. Mix in cheese just before serving.

Makes 6-7 cups.

PETER'S FAVORITE

Another one of our very simple dishes, enjoyed many evenings by lakes and in the shadow of pines.

Weigh each ingredient and bag together:

> 8 oz beef-flavored soy nuggets
> 1 oz dehydrated green peppers
> 1 oz or 2 cubes beef bouillon
> 8 oz noodles

Bag separately:

> 10 oz sour cream mix

In camp:

Heat about 6 cups of water, and when it begins to simmer add the contents of the first bag. Cover the pot and continue to simmer, stirring from time to time, for about 20 minutes. When noodles test done, or tender, add the sour cream (reconstituted with cool water). Check seasoning and serve.

Serves 4, about 2 Sierra cups each.

SPAGHETTI WITH/WITHOUT MEATBALLS

This familiar and hearty meal is good with soy beef or freeze-dried meatballs. We've carried it along both ways, often.

Weigh and bag together:

> 8 oz beef-flavored soy nuggets or
>> 1 pkg freeze-dried meatballs
> 1 oz or 2 cubes beef bouillon
> ½ oz dried onion, or more if you really like it
> 9-10 oz spaghetti, broken into 3 in. pieces

Bag separately:

> 4 oz tomato crystals

Also take:

> 1 pkg spaghetti sauce mix
> 3 or 4 oz grated Parmesan cheese

Assemble all these bags and packets in one dinner bag.

In camp:
  Bring 6 cups of water to a simmer and add the contents of the first bag. Blend tomato crystals with cool water in a chain shaker or cup. When pot has simmered about 20 minutes, blend in sauce mix and tomato paste. Continue cooking until spaghetti is tender. Serve with cheese.
  Makes 8 or 9 Sierra cups.

GREEN GOULASH

A tin of roast beef can be substituted for the freeze-dried beef or TVP in our recipes, but the tin must come out with you, to prevent a bad aftertaste for all.

Package together:

> 2 oz freeze-dried beef or
>> 4 oz beef-flavored TVP granules
> 8 oz spinach-flavored noodles
> 2 oz tomato crystals
> 4 cubes beef bouillon or ¼ cup bouillon granules
> 1 tsp each basil, paprika
> ¼ cup dried bell peppers
> 1 envelope cream of onion soup mix, making
>> 2½ cups soup

To prepare:

Bring 7 cups water to boil. Add noodle-meat mixture and simmer 10 minutes. Meanwhile mix ½ cup cold water into soup. Add soup to pot, cook 5-10 minutes longer, or until noodles and meat are tender. If using canned roast beef, reduce bouillon by half. Sour cream mix stirred in just before serving makes another good variation.

Makes about 8 cups.

ELEGANT CHICKEN IN SOUR CREAM

And very easy to fix, too.

Package together:

> 2 oz freeze-dried chicken or
>> 4 oz chicken-flavored TVP
> 4 cubes chicken bouillon or ¼ cup bouillon granules
> 8 oz enriched pasta
> 1 tsp dill weed

Also include, in separate packets:

> 1 envelope cream of onion soup mix, making
>> 2½ cups soup
> 8 oz sour cream mix
> ½ cup sliced almonds
> 1-2 oz freeze-dried peas

To prepare:

Heat 7 cups water to boiling, add pasta-chicken mix, and simmer, stirring occasionally for 10 minutes. Meanwhile mix about ½ cup water with soup. Pour into pot, stirring, and simmer 5-10 minutes more, or until pasta and chicken are tender. Peas should be cooked with chicken for amount of time recommended on their package. Reconstitute sour cream mix with cold water, stir into pot. Serve, sprinkling almonds on top of each cup.

Makes about 8 cups.

DINNER OMELET

The ubiquitous egg is welcome any time of day.

In one bag:

> 1 cup whole dried egg
> ¼ cup whole dried milk
> 1 tsp salt

Also take:

> 1 pkg freeze-dried ham dices
> 2 or 3 slices of cheddar cheese
> from the lunch cheeses

To prepare:

Rehydrate ham in its packet. Mix egg/milk with 2 cups of water, blending well to avoid lumps. Melt 1 or 2 tbsp of margarine in frypan, and when it's bubbling pour in the egg mixture. Drain ham and sprinkle it over the eggs. Cook gently as you do scrambled eggs. When the eggs are almost done, lower the heat and arrange cheese slices over the top of the egg mixture. Remove from heat and cover pan. Let it stand a minute or two to melt the cheese.

Serves 4.

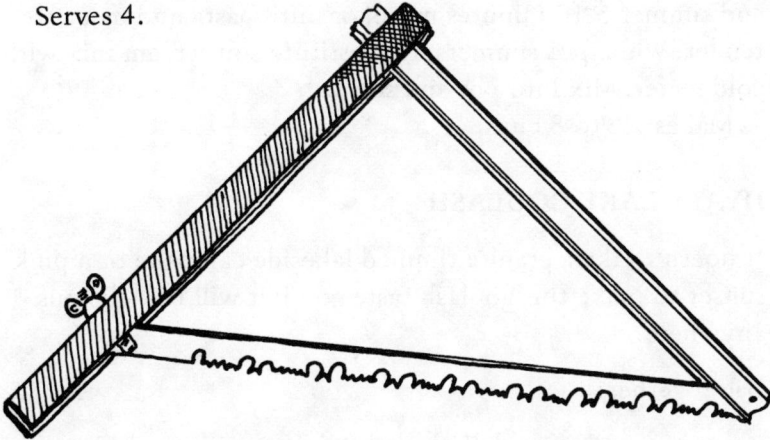

A FOLDING SAW

BEEF STROGANOFF

It's a long way from linen, crystal, and silverware to your battered camp cups and spoons, but the dish retains much elegance, even in a rain-soaked tent.

Bag together:

> 2 oz freeze-dried beef chunks or
>   4 oz beef-flavored TVP
> 4 beef bouillon cubes or ¼ cup bouillon granules
> ½ cup freeze-dried mushroom slices
> 2 tbsp instant minced onion
> ⅛ tsp garlic powder
> 8 oz enriched pasta

Put this in a bag with:

> 1 envelope cream of mushroom soup mix
> 8 oz sour cream mix in a separate bag

To prepare:

Heat 7 cups water to boiling. Add pasta-beef mix and simmer, stirring occasionally for about 10 minutes. Meanwhile mix about ½ cup water with soup. Pour into pot, stirring, and simmer 5-10 minutes more, or until pasta and meat are tender. While pot simmers, reconstitute sour cream mix with cold water. Mix into pot and serve.

Makes 7½ to 8 cups.

HYATT LAKE GOULASH

It doesn't take a granite-rimmed lakeside campsite or a pink sunset to make this goulash taste good; it will be delicious anywhere.

Bag together:

> 1 oz dehydrated onion
> 6 oz dehydrated potato shreds
> 1 pkg puff-dried carrot slices

120

Take, packaged separately:

> 1 pkg freeze-dried beef dices
> 2 slices bacon or 1 tbsp bacon bar
> ½ cup dehydrated sour cream
> 2 oz tomato crystals

Bag together:

> 1 tbsp flour
> ¼ tsp paprika
> ½ tsp garlic powder
> 1 oz beef bouillon
> 1 tsp marjoram
> 1 tbsp parsley flakes

In a small plastic bottle:

> **About 1 oz Worcestershire sauce**

Assemble all these bags and packets in one bag.

To prepare:

Cook bacon, or bacon bar, first. When bacon is done, take it out, but keep the fat. If you've used bacon bar, you may want to add a spoonful of margarine. While the bacon is cooking, rehydrate onions. Add the onions, potatoes, and carrots to the fat and very carefully pour in about 4 cups of hot water. Simmer until these vegetables are almost tender. While the vegetables are simmering, rehydrate the beef in its packet; blend the tomato crystals into a paste with cool water; and mix the sour cream with enough cool water to make a paste. When vegetables are almost tender, add beef, bacon, and tomato sauce to the potatoes and blend well. Then add the contents of the last bag—flour and seasonings. Simmer till mixture thickens. Taste and correct seasonings, adding Worcestershire sauce. Finally, add sour cream and heat for a minute or two.

Makes 8 Sierra cups.

PACKBAG PAELLA

This Spanish dish is traditionally flavored with saffron. If you own and use this costly flavoring, by all means add a bit to the spice bag for this dish. Even without it, it's a mighty tasty dish.

Take:

> 2 oz freeze-dried shrimp, 2 oz freeze-dried chicken, and ½ oz freeze-dried ham, or substitute canned shrimp, and soy ham and chicken

Bag together:

> 1 tbsp dried onion
> 2 tbsp dried green peppers
> 2 tsp chicken bouillon crystals
> 1 tsp basil
> ¼ tsp garlic powder
> 1 tsp paprika

Bag separately:

> ½ cup tomato crystals
> ½ oz freeze-dried peas
> 1 cup quick brown or converted rice

Put all small bags and packets in one large bag.

In camp:
Presoak all freeze-dried foods, following package directions. Measure 3½ cups water into pot, bring to a boil, and add rice, onions, and all seasonings. When the rice is tender and most of the liquid absorbed, add the freeze-dried items. Heat for a few minutes, check seasoning, and serve.
Makes 8 Sierra cups.

Note: If you decide to use the soy meats, remember they need to cook right along with the rice and will also need some added water to rehydrate.

A super-quick version of this dish can be made using all freeze-dried items where you can, and minute rice. Simply presoak the freeze-dried foods as your normally would. Then add rice, seasonings, and water to the presoaked items, bring to a simmer, and cook for about 10 minutes. Remove from heat, cover, and let stand a few minutes till water is absorbed and rice is tender.

DESSERT

HONEST-TO-CHOCOLATE PUDDING

Real pudding takes about the same cooking time as the packaged ones do and it's full of rich flavors and honest nourishment—no additives here.

Measure and bag:

> **1 cup whole dry milk**
> **2 squares unsweetened chocolate**

Measure, mix together, and bag in another bag:

> **3 tbsp cornstarch**
> **⅓ cup sugar**
> **¼ tsp salt**
> **2 tbsp whole dry milk**

Note on bag 1—"Add 2 cups hot water."
Note on bag 2—"Add ¼ cup cold water, blend into hot milk, cook till thick."

Measure about 1 tsp vanilla, rum, or sherry into one of those tiny plastic screw-top bottles. Add just before serving.

Serves about 4 Sierra cups.

APRICOT SQUASH

In one small bag measure:

> ½ cup brown sugar
> ½ cup chopped Virginia peanuts

Also take separately:

> 1 packet lemon crystals
> ½ lb dried apricot halves
> 3 tbsp margarine, added to general supply
> ¼ cup bourbon whisky

To prepare:

Rehydrate apricots in hot water, drain. Mix them with all the rest of the ingredients and heat very gently over a low heat or a bed of hot coals. Watch it carefully so it doesn't burn on the bottom. Heat till sugar is bubbly. If you are carrying a reflector oven, bake it in the cake pan until nicely heated through.

Serves 4.

A SWISS ARMY KNIFE

DESSERT OMELET

If dinner has been a little light on protein, why not make it up with this luscious sweet?

Bag together:

> 1 cup whole dried egg
> ¼ cup dried milk
> 1 tsp salt

In a second bag:

> ½ cup sour cream mix

In a third bag:

> ½ cup evaporated apples
> ½ tsp cinnamon

To prepare:

Simmer apples with about 1 cup water and the cinnamon until they're tender. Check package directions to see if adding sugar is recommended; this varies with different products. Blend sour cream mix with cool water to make a thick paste. Prepare egg mixture with 2 cups of water and cook in 1 or 2 tbsp margarine in pot lid or frypan. Try to keep the cooked egg in a solid mass. When the egg is done, spread half the sour cream on half the egg. Spoon some of the applesauce over the sour cream. Fold egg over and spoon on remaining sauce and cream.

Makes about 4 servings.

GINGERBREAD PANCAKES

These are irresistably good either after a light dinner or for breakfast. Eat plain, with margarine, with applesauce, with marmalade and/or sour cream, or with lemon pudding sauce from a mix.

Stir together and bag:

> 1½ cups whole-wheat flour
> ⅔ cup powdered whole egg
> ⅓ cup sugar
> 2 tsp baking powder
> 1 tsp ginger
> ½ tsp coriander
> ¼ tsp salt

Carry in plastic tube:

> ⅔ cup molasses

Include in general supply:

> ¼ cup margarine

To prepare:

Heat margarine and molasses with ½ cup water until margarine melts. Stir into flour mixture to make a fairly thin batter, adding more water as necessary. Bake 2-inch cakes on a greased griddle over a slow fire.

Or, if you'd rather, carry a package of complete gingerbread mix. Thin to proper consistency with water and bake as directed.

APPLE CRISP

If you are carrying a reflector oven, bake this dessert for
about half an hour in it. If you're not, set it to cook over
a very low fire in your frypan.

Measure and bag:

> ¾ cup evaporated apples

Measure, blend together, and bag:

> ¾ cup flour
> ¾ cup brown sugar
> ½ tsp cinnamon
> ½ cup margarine

In camp:

Simmer apples in water according to package directions.
When they are well heated, but not completely cooked, add
the sugar/flour mixture and spread in a pot lid or frypan.
Continue cooking until mixture is bubbly and thickened.
Although this dessert will be just as tasty, it will not have
the brown crust associated with baked apple crisp.

If you do bake the apple crisp, spread the apples in your
reflector oven pan and pat the flour/sugar mixture over them.
Bake in front of a good high fire, turning the pan once or
twice to assure even baking.

Serves about 6 Sierra cups.

TRAIL-BAKED

SWEET THINGS

MASTER MIX

A bag of mix hidden in your pack and a few flavorings can instantly be transformed into delicious—and nutritious—baked goodies for perking jaded palates.

> 4 cups sifted enriched, unbleached flour
> and ½ cup soy flour, or 4 cups
> whole-wheat flour
> 1½ tsp salt
> 2 tbsp baking powder
> 1 cup powdered skim milk
> 1 cup powdered whole egg
> 1 cup margarine

Thoroughly combine dry ingredients in a bowl. Cut in margarine as for pastry. Use mix within a week, or refrigerate for longer storage.

Makes about 8½ cups.

BISCUITS

2 cups mix, ½ cup water. Makes about 15 two-inch biscuits, rolled or patted ¼ inch thick. Bake in reflector oven or in frying pan over slow fire as for scones, turning once.

Flavor the biscuits with ½ to 1 tsp herb or spice, 1 tbsp instant minced onion, raisins, crumbled cheese or bacon bar, or bacon-flavored bits.

COFFEECAKE

2 cups mix, ½ tsp cardamom or coriander, ½ cup sugar,
¾ cup water. Pour into greased pan, distribute topping,
pour over 3 tbsp melted margarine. Bake in reflector oven.
Toppings:
    Jam from plastic tube, or
    ½ cup brown sugar, ¼ cup sesame seeds or chopped nuts,
        ¼ tsp lemon peel, or
    ½ cup Breakfast Gorp (page 68) or Apple Jack Gorp
        (page 69)

DUMPLINGS

See page 101.

PANCAKES

2 cups mix, 1 cup water. Makes about 30 two-inch pancakes.
Variations: Add ½ cup cornmeal, a little more water. Add
½ cup chopped nuts or raisins.

ORANGE-SESAME CAKE
Reflector oven

> 1½ cups whole-wheat flour
> ½ cup soy flour
> 1 tsp salt
> 2 tsp baking powder
> ¼ cup sesame seeds
> ¼ cup whole dried egg
> 2 tbsp grated orange peel
> ½ cup sugar
> ½ cup margarine

Blend all the above ingredients thoroughly, using the low
speed of the electric mixer. Pour mixture into a bag and
close the top securely.

At the campsite:
    Grease the baking pan of your reflector oven with mar-

garine. Check to be sure the fire is burning well and that
you have a reserve of wood. Blend ¾ cup of water into the
mix and blend to make a stiff batter. A few lumps are okay.
Spread batter in pan and bake about 30 minutes or till it's
done. Remember, start with the oven back from the fire
and gradually bring it closer for browning.

    Serves 4.

DATE PUDDING
Reflector oven

Cut up:

> 1½ cups dates

Bag in a small bag and label—"+ 1 cup hot water, 1 tbsp
margarine."

Into a second bag, measure:

> 1 cup sugar
> 1½ cup flour
> 1 tsp baking soda
> ½ tsp salt
> ½ cup chopped nuts

Close both bags with twist ties securely.

To prepare:
    Pour hot water on dates and let them soak during dinner.
Margarine will melt in the hot water, too. Grease the baking
pan of your reflector oven with margarine. Stir the dates
into the dry ingredients until all is well blended. Spread this
batter evenly over the pan. Begin baking this cake with the
oven back a little from the full heat of the fire. Gradually
move it closer for even browning. With a good fire this will
be done in about 30 minutes.
    Serves 4 about 2½-inch-square pieces.

BROWNIES
Reflector oven

At home, in the large bowl of an electric mixer, blend together:

> ½ cup margarine
> 1 cup granulated sugar
> ¼ cup whole dried egg
> ¼ cup + 2 tbsp carob powder
> ¾ cup whole-wheat flour
> 2 tbsp wheat germ
> ¼ tsp salt
> ½ cup chopped nuts

Bag this mixture and label—"+ ¾ cup water, blend well."

At the campsite:

Blend mix with water to form a stiff batter. Spread batter evenly in greased reflector oven pan. Be sure fire is burning well. Start baking with oven away from the most intense heat and gradually move it closer as batter begins to bake. Brownies will be done in about half an hour.

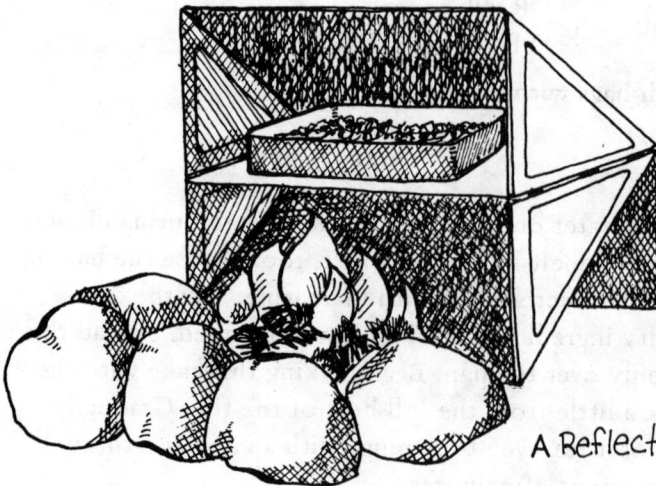

A Reflector Oven

TRAIL BREAKFAST/DESSERT CAKE

Equally delicious morning or evening, this very simple cake is just Master Mix plus Breakfast Gorp.

Measure and bag together:

> 2 cups Master Mix
> ½ cup granulated sugar

Measure and bag separately, or add to the general supply:

> 3 tbsp margarine
> 1¼ cup Breakfast Gorp
> (including brown sugar)

In camp:

Arrange a good hot fire and grease the reflector oven pan very thoroughly with margarine. Melt 3 tbsp margarine in a Sierra cup near the fire. Add about half to the Master Mix and blend well. Then stir in about ¾ cup water, adding it a little at a time to allow the dehydrated ingredients to absorb enough water to rehydrate. When batter seems well blended, spread it in the pan and sprinkle the Breakfast Gorp over the top. Drizzle the last of the melted margarine over Gorp and begin baking.

If the fire is hot and steady, it will take about 30 minutes to bake. This cake served with cocoa will provide a good high-calorie breakfast for four hikers. If there are six in the party, or four very large appetites, serve with an omelet.

BEVERAGES

FOR ALL TIMES

OF DAY

HIKER'S COCOA I

>   ¾ cup powdered unsweetened cocoa
>   1 cup sugar
>   2¾ cups powdered instant skim milk, or
>   2 envelopes Milkman, or 2 cups whole
>   dry milk
>   1 tsp salt

Put everything into a container with a tight-fitting lid. Shake very vigorously to blend.

   We use a scant 1/3 cup of this mix to make one 8 oz cup of rich-tasting chocolate. Usually we use the instant non-fat dry milk. Try this at home, as the perfect proportion for you may be a bit more or a bit less of the mix to water.

HIKER'S COCOA II

>   1 cup commercially mixed sweetened cocoa
>   2 cups whole dry milk

Blend thoroughly as above. We use 2 heaping spoonfuls for each 8 oz cup. This is a less chocolatey but high fat calorie drink. In either case, once you've settled on your blend, simply multiply by the number of servings to find out how much you'll need for a trip. If you are using non-instant milk, be sure to add the water gradually to avoid lumping. We often use the chain shaker to form a milk paste first.

TRAIL MILK SHAKES

A good variety of prepackaged milk shake drinks is available in backpacking stores and various "instant breakfast" products can be found in the supermarkets. However, there are several interesting possibilities when you make your own.

BASIC MIX FOR ONE SERVING

> ½ cup whole dry milk (for more fat), or
>   non-fat dry milk (more protein)
> 1 tbsp flavoring
> ¼ tsp gum tragacanth (thickening) or
>   1 tbsp malted milk powder

Fill the one-cup size chain shaker with cool water, shake and serve.

Flavorings:
> Blueberry syrup mix
> Cocoa or carob + ¼ tsp pumpkin pie spice
> Instant coffee
> Kool-aide fruit flavors
> Fruit jam
> Rum, sherry

HIGH-PROTEIN MILK SHAKE

> ½ cup non-fat dry milk
> 1 tbsp dry egg white
> 1 tbsp flavoring
> 1 tbsp malted milk powder

Shake with cool water and serve.

LONG, COOL DRINKS

You may be lucky and camp by a snowbank, who knows?

LEMON-LIME SWIZZLE

Prepare a package of lemon-lime drink mix according to package directions. Add rum if you wish, and sprinkle with a pinch of dried mint leaves.

BLOODY HARRY

> ½ oz tomato crystals for each drink
> A small plastic bottle of Worcestershire sauce
> Several packets of lemon crystals

Blend the tomato crystals with cold water and pour into cups. Let each drinker add Worcestershire sauce or lemon crystals or vodka to taste.

NEARLY WINE COOLER

Grape-flavored drink crystals (Tang). Blend with cold water and add vodka to taste.

TEA BLENDS

PUNGENT AND SPICY

> 1 cup orange pekoe tea
> ⅓ cup orange spice tea
>   (Constant Comment or others)
> ⅓ cup Earl Grey tea

Blend together in a bowl until thoroughly mixed. Spoon into a bag and tie tightly.

REFRESHING MINT

> ¾ cup orange pekoe tea
> ¼ cup dried peppermint leaves

Blend together in a bowl. Pour into a bag and tie tightly.

At the campsite:

Bring several cups of water to a boil. Fill a small tea ball about ¾ full and drop it into the rapidly boiling water. Immediately take the pot off the fire and let it stand, covered, several minutes to develop the flavor of the tea.

One standard measuring cup full of tea weighs about 4 oz and will provide enough tea for about 40 cups. Those who like very strong tea may want to use more, of course, and some very fine teas will weigh less.

GOOD BOOKS, GUIDES, AND SOURCES

*To read true books in a true spirit is a
noble exercise...*
—Henry Thoreau, *Walden*

GOOD BOOKS ABOUT BACKPACKING

For your convenience, we've used the list as it appears in the
Moor & Mountain catalog, page 49. All may be ordered from
them; many are also available in local bookstores.

The Packrat Papers No. 1. Cameron (1972) 51 pages
   Collected hints on clothing, equipment and whatnot from
   the pages of "Signpost," a newsletter for hikers and back-
   packers.
Appalachian Hiker. Edward B. Garvey (1970) 397 pages
   A completely documented account of hiking the Trail
   from Georgia to Maine.
The Backpacker. Albert and Gompers Saijo (1972) 96 pages
   This common-sense guide to backpacking in the wilderness
   outlines the basic requirements in straightforward, up-to-
   date terms.
Backcountry Camping. Riviere (1971) 320 pages
   General introductory guide to all forms of camping from
   backpacking to canoe tripping, weekend outings to
   extended trips.

Backpacking. Rethmel, R. C. (1972) 122 pages
A methodical treatment of all aspects of backpacking technique and equipment intended to be a complete reference guide. Spiral-bound typescript 8½ inches by 11 inches, with offset photos.

The Hiker's and Backpacker's Handbook. Merrill (1971) 320 pages. For beginners.

Backpack Techniques. Ruth Ayar Mendenhall (1967) 36 pages. For beginners.

Sierra Club Wilderness Handbook. David Brower, editor (rev. March 1971) 234 pages. General information for the beginner.

Reading the Woods. Vinson Brown (1969) 160 pages Backpacker's and camper's guide to botany, geology, and ecology.

The Complete Walker. Colin Fletcher (1968) 353 pages America's most famous walker has written this practical, personal, comprehensive handbook for anyone planning a simple overnight journey or an extended trip on foot into the wilderness.

Backpacking: One Step at a Time. Harvey Manning (1972) 375 pages. A new book aimed at the novice by the editor of "Mountaineering, Freedom of the Hills." A very solid text.

Pleasure Packing. Robert Wood (1972) 213 pages Well-organized, competent, detailed treatment of all aspects of backpacking by an experienced practitioner.

GUIDES FOR GOOD NUTRITION

Agriculture Handbook No. 8. USDA, Revised December 1963, Washington, D.C.

Food, The Yearbook of Agriculture 1959. USDA, Washington, D.C.

Composition of Foods. Bernice K. Watt and Annabel L. Merrill.

MAIL ORDER FOOD PEOPLE

These are primarily suppliers of an enormous variety of dried and freeze-dried foods, both in bulk and in smaller amounts.

Perma-Pak
40 East 2430 South
Salt Lake City, Utah 84115

FSP Foods
P. O. Box 6128
Albany, California 94706

These are manufacturers of freeze-dried foods intended primarily for backpackers.

Ad Seidel & Son, Inc.
2323 Pratt Boulevard
Elk Grove Village, Illinois 60007

Richmoor
P. O. Box 2728
Van Nuys, California 91404

Dri-Lite Foods
8716 Santa Fe Avenue
Southgate, California 90280

MOUNTAINEERING SUPPLIERS

Just a sampling of mail order outfitters who offer a good selection of freeze-dried foods and cooking gear.

Moor & Mountain
Main Street
Concord, Massachusetts 01742

Recreational Equipment, Inc.
1525 - 11th Avenue
Seattle, Washington 98122

Holubar
P. O. Box 7
Boulder, Colorado 80302

Coop Wilderness Supply
47 Tamal Vista Boulevard
Corte Madera, California 94925

Ski Hut
1615 University Avenue
Berkeley, California 94703

The Mountain Shop
228 Grant Avenue
San Francisco, California 94108

Eastern Mountain Sports
1041 Commonwealth Avenue
Boston, Massachusetts 02215